BLIND
SPOT

War and
Christian Identity

BLIND
SPOT

War and Christian Identity

Second Edition

Dorothy Garrity Ranaghan

New City Press
Hyde Park, New York

Published in the United States by New City Press
202 Comforter Blvd., Hyde Park, NY 12538
www.newcitypress.com
©2018 Dorothy Garrity Ranaghan

Cover design by Miguel Tejerina

Blind Spot Second Edition: War and Christian Identity /
Dorothy Garrity Ranaghan.

Library of Congress Cataloging Control Number:
2018945345

ISBN: 978-1-56548-663-8 (paperback)
ISBN:978-1-56548-664-5 (e-book)

Printed in the United States of America

To Kevin:
my wise, humorous and beloved friend / husband

Blind Spot . . . condenses a lifetime of wisdom garnered from theologians, exegetes, spiritual writers and peace activists. . . . Ms. Ranaghan's small book provides a path into the mind of the church on peace and war today.

Drew Christiansen, S.J
Distinguished Professor of Ethics and
Global Human Development
Georgetown University, Drew Christiansen, S.J.
Distinguished Professor of Ethics and Global
Human Development Georgetown University

"*Blind Spot* is a remarkable book — well-written and totally engaging."

Charles Whitehead
Past Chairman, National Service Committee
for the Charismatic Renewal in England

"In this well-researched and well-reasoned book, Dorothy Ranaghan challenges us and offers healing for a major blind spot in our contemporary understanding of the teachings of the church and scripture on war and violence."

Bert Ghezzi
Author of Voices of the Saints: A 365-Day Journey
with our Spiritual Companions

Contents

Preface

Blind Spot: War and Christian Identity

Reflecting on the fall of Communism in Eastern Europe through the nonviolent revolutions of 1989, Saint John Paul II concluded with this aspiration: "May people learn to fight for justice without violence, renouncing class struggle in their internal dispute[s] and war in international ones."

Pope John Paul took nonviolence seriously, devoting three paragraphs in *Centesimus annus*—nos. 23, 25, and 52—to the topic, with perhaps the most trenchant critique of war to be found in modern Catholic Social Teaching (no. 52), and one of the most compelling spiritual interpretations of Christian nonviolence (no. 23). In part, he wrote,

It is by uniting his own sufferings for truth and freedom to the suffering of Christ on the Cross that man is able to accomplish the miracle of peace and is in a position to discern the narrow path between the cowardice which gives in to evil and the violence, which under the illusion of fighting evil, only makes it worse (no. 25).

"[T]he violence, which under the illusion of fighting evil, only makes it worse" suggests the "blind spot" that Dorothy Garrity Ranaghan identifies and explores.

Pope John Paul made very limited allowance for war to defend against injustice; he did not consider himself a pacifist. For her part, Ms. Ranaghan would call herself a pacifist because she considers war to be incompatible with Christian existence. A charismatic Catholic and a longtime member of the South Bend ecumenical covenant community People of Praise, she believes that the re-birth of Christians through baptism requires that they act in the world like Christ—nonviolently. Likewise, connected to the Catholic Worker and the Catholic Peace Fellowship, both active in South Bend, she presents community prayer and peace witness as essential to Christian life.

Among her heroes are Dorothy Day, whose presence converted Ranaghan to nonviolence when they met at Duquesne University. Another is Joshua Casteel, a West Point graduate and Iraq War veteran who converted to Catholicism and pacifism while serving as an interrogator at Abu Ghraib. After he was separated from the military as a conscientious objector, Casteel became a writer and speaker, but died young from illnesses he contracted while burning toxic trash outside the Abu Ghraib compound. Joshua and his disabled and deceased G.I. comrades are among those Saint John Paul regarded as the victims of war:

No, never again war, which destroys the lives of innocent people, teaches how to kill, [and] throws into upheaval the lives of those who do the killing . . .

Joshua's death in 2012 exemplifies what we have learned about the damage war inflicts on those who wage it: physical trauma, PTSD, moral injury—obsessive feelings of guilt for deeds of war some consider morally permissible—the indignity in having to justify healthcare for damage done at the behest of their government and fellow citizens. Despite their sacrifices, many have become the discards, in Pope Francis' famous phrase, of "our throwaway culture."

General readers will find *Blind Spot* a personal chapbook on Christian peacemaking, a slim volume that condenses a lifetime of wisdom garnered from theologians, exegetes, spiritual writers and peace activists. It provides a helpful survey of how Catholic and ecumenical Christian thinking on peace and war have been evolving since the U.S. bishops' 1983 pastoral letter, "The Challenge of Peace." It will assist readers in understanding the full import of Pope John Paul's oracular statement that nonviolent activists must discern the difference between the cowardice of submission to injustice and "the violence, which under the illusion of fighting evil, only makes it worse." They may also begin to grasp what the U.S. bishops affirmed in their 1993 pastoral, "The Harvest of Justice Is Sown in Peace": "In situations of conflict, our constant commitment ought to be, as far as possible, to strive for justice through nonviolent means." Ms. Ranaghan's small book provides a path into the mind of the church on peace and war today.

Drew Christiansen, S.J.
Distinguished Professor of Ethics
and Global Human Development
Georgetown University
18 July 2018

I

Prophetic Discomfort

"They carried the same Bible. They believed in the same God. One side fought for God's glory, the other for His Kingdom on Earth. But for the duration of the war, God refused to take sides."[1]

The trailer for *Gods and Generals*, which focuses upon the devoutly religious "Stonewall" Jackson, opens with these words. What follows in this Civil War movie is bloodshed. Believers all. Watching it left me with disturbing questions. Does God have a "side" in any war? How can one tell? Should a Christian take up arms to smite the enemy? Should other Christians be the enemy? Are there answers to these questions?

In a March 6, 2018 article for the Catholic New Service, Mark Pattison reported that a 2018 Pew Research poll of United States Catholics noted "signs of growing discontent with Pope Francis among Catholics on the political right." The survey, he said, reflects the fact that political leanings affect the approval ratings of the pope.[2] The same reality seems to be happening among Catholics regarding war or gun control or immigration. The pope, the councils

---

1. *Gods and Generals*, dir. Ronald F. Maxwell, Warner Brothers, 2003.
2. Mark Pattison. "U.S. Catholics' Political Leanings Affect Their Approval Ratings of Pope," https://cnstopstories.com/2018/03/06/u-s-catholics-political-leanings-affect-their-approval-ratings-of-pope/.

of bishops, even the Bible seem to have less influence on worldview and "opinions" than political leaders. If, despite condemnation by Church leaders, those political officials decide preemptively to use nuclear bombs on North Korea or any other place, I fear that many would capitulate to that line of thinking. It is a dangerous blind spot.

Many Christians have a collective blind spot concerning the culture of war. I use the image of a blind spot to suggest what may be lacking in our understanding, because I know the distortion a blind spot can cause. In July, 2006, in my left eye appeared a big yellow dot surrounded by a black jagged edge. I could read only by shifting my vision to the edges. The ophthalmologist had me look at a printed grid and asked if I could see the center dot. I could not, and the surrounding lines looked like worms. Further tests revealed that I had a large "macular hole," a gap in the retina.

Because of my "blind spot," a hole in the center of my vision, I could not see a whole range of things. In a similar way, I have found that many Christians have a blind spot—theological or practical—when it comes to issues of war and violence, and that inability to see seems to stem from a hole in our vision of Christian identity. Healing is needed.

Shock and Awe. Fire and Fury. These words strike excitement in the hearts and minds of many Americans eager for payback and revenge in the wake of atrocities. Sadly, many Christians as well experience those sentiments. But such sentiments fly in the face of the Gospel. It is the meek who will inherit the earth. Swords must be turned into plowshares; we must forgive them for they know not what they do. Ah but this "turn the other cheek" mentality is doomed, we hear. Perhaps. Are we then saying the Lord is a fool or at least naive? It is my unpopular opinion that accepting the drumbeat of war rhetoric risks weakening our understanding of the faith, even may be blasphemous.

Each person can speak only from his or her own experience. I myself speak as a lifelong Catholic who during her formative years experienced the ferment of biblical and liturgical renewal that preceded the Second Vatican Council. The power, insight, and enthusiasm of those days prepared me for the movement of the Holy Spirit in the charismatic renewal, a potent Pentecostal reality that has defined and shaped my life and the lives of millions of other Catholics around the world. Where that movement of God has achieved its intent and purpose, it has also led Catholics, Protestants, Pentecostals, Orthodox and non-denominational Christians into the broader, historic, twentieth century ecumenical movement. Brought together by the power of the Spirit in loving cooperation, they have come to realize that what unites them is greater than what divides them.

For me it has also meant, since 1971, entering and maintaining a covenant with brothers and sisters in an ecumenical, charismatic, community called the People of Praise. We are not a prayer group, but a community of life. Our permanent commitment resembles what Christian religious orders and other intentional communities also make. We are Methodists and Lutherans, Roman Catholics and Pentecostals, Baptists and Episcopalians. For the most part we are lay Christians—married couples, children and single people; a few are ordained Roman Catholic and Lutheran clergy. As our website[3] explains, The People of Praise Christian community is part of a global movement

_____

3.   https://peopleofpraise.org/about/who-we-are/charismatic

that has brought powerful new experiences of the Holy Spirit to more than 500 million people since the beginning of the twentieth century It is a community where Christians from diverse church backgrounds can share life, work, prayer and mission while still maintaining active membership in their local congregations. After a long period of prayer and participation in community life, many members of the People of Praise choose to make a lifelong commitment to the community—a covenant. Today we continue to experience the awesome power of the Holy Spirit in our lives. Together as a community we exercise the spiritual gifts in our prayer. Throughout our daily lives, the Holy Spirit inspires us and helps us solve problems large and small. He empowers us in our work as mothers and fathers, teachers and students, missionaries, caregivers, pastors and business people. Every year we see more and more lives transformed by the baptism of the Holy Spirit. As a community, and together with the whole Church, we pray for a continued outpouring of the Holy Spirit in our time, so that all men and women might come to know, love and serve Jesus.

This is my world and my worldview. It is also the world I wish to address first, because most of my fellow Catholics, other charismatics, even most of the brothers and sisters in my own community defend a Christian's right (many believe it a duty) to participate in warfare. With the urgency of a **prophetic call**, therefore, I submit these reflections as an attempt to confront the Christian attitude toward war, to clarify and to enlighten. In these days when phrases like "shock and awe"[4] and "fire and

---

4. "Shock and awe," also known as "rapid dominance," is a military strategy of using overwhelming power and massive displays of force to intimidate

fury"[5] have entered popular vocabulary, perhaps a growing uneasiness with violence may lead us to rethink our
response to warfare.

**In particular, we need to re-examine the Christian
response to *modern* warfare.** Past decisions, past or current "conventional" wars, or viewpoints on war in general
must be set aside because the nuclear option changes the
nature of the conversation. Examining political ideologies
that served a useful purpose in a non-nuclear age may be
disconcerting, but discomfort may be appropriate. For
example, to many the war of words between the leader
of North Korea and the president of the United States on
the strength and size of their respective nuclear options is
more than discomfiting. It instills great fear.

In 1991, days after the Persian Gulf War began, our
neighborhood was awash in red, white and blue, almost
every home flying an American flag. A palpable patriotism
swept over our neighborhood, and our country. Some did
object to the "war," however; one commentator analyzed
public reaction as a contest of "patriots versus pacifists."
The way he characterized the opinions on such a crucial
issue saddened me. Rhetoric like his only widened the
rift between those whose Christianity accepts advancing
national purpose through military power and those who
espouse gospel-based nonviolence. A lot has happened
since then: Iraq, Afghanistan, Syria, the battle with ISIS.
The polarization of viewpoints on the use of military
power has only increased.

---

opponents and destroy their will to fight.

5.   Used by President Donald Trump to threaten bombing in response to
      bellicose comments by the leader of North Korea.

Polarization is not new. In 1968, tension and passionate disagreement on the morality of the Vietnam War was common. "Peaceniks" were ridiculed. Yet to be ridiculed was, and is, better than to be ignored, as dissenters were in 1991. In times of crisis, dissenting voices are often seen as inconvenient, or irrelevant. I am neither a total patriot nor a total pacifist. Those terms need not be considered contradictory. My ultimate concern is neither patriotism nor pacifism, but the gospel of Jesus Christ.

Even a cursory reading of history indicates that Christians have not always agreed on what the gospel demands on the issues of violence and war. Jesus said (Mt 5:39) that if someone strikes you on the right cheek, turn the other as well. Most Christians strive to follow this "ethic," but face agonizing division as they seek to apply their personal ethical principles to international conflicts. I acknowledge that there are no simple solutions. Yet, to use a phrase from popular jargon, the Lord has "raised my consciousness."

In 1991, I traveled to Brighton, England, to attend an international, inter-racial, interdenominational congress on world evangelization. For a week, Orthodox, Catholic, Protestant, Pentecostal and non-denominational charismatic Christian leaders from over 100 countries talked, ate, and worshipped together. Because it was held shortly after the fall of the Berlin Wall and the opening of Eastern Europe, Christians from Russia, Hungary, Poland, and many other countries that previously had banned travel to such gatherings were able to attend. In that context I became convicted that our unity in Christ with these brothers and sisters from all over the world was stronger than any enmity our countries engaged in. War with their countries might even mean killing these people. Unthinkable.

In a multinational, multicultural, multiracial gathering like the Brighton Conference on evangelization other truths began to surface. Eating dinner with an Orthodox brother and sister from Moscow; embracing one brother from a non-denominational church in Iraq and another from Iran; listening to stories of faith from China, Korea, the Philippines, Latin America, and the many African nations; watching Protestants and Catholics from Northern Ireland meet and talk; or sharing a laugh with a Palestinian Catholic and a Messianic Jew makes real and tangible the truth that all of us Christians are loyal to the same king. Our enmities have been reconciled in his blood, blood that has made us one family, one people, one "holy nation." This is our true nationhood. Geoffrey Nuttall, a former lecturer in Church history at New College in Oxford once noted that wherever Christians work together on the international level, they realize that they are brothers and sisters in Christ and find that when they return home it becomes "inconceivable to prepare measures of war against one another."[6]

By discussing and planning evangelization on a global level, it becomes more and more clear that while God can bring good out of anything, the non Christian world cannot be brought to see the love of Jesus while Christians conduct bombing raids against them. The late Monika Hellwig, a Catholic theologian at Georgetown University, questioned how Christians can claim to understand the nature, purpose and power of the Eucharist while they engage in war, especially in poor countries. "The Eucharist of Christian community celebrates the liberating power of

---

6.   Geoffrey Nuttall, *Christian Pacifism in History* (Berkeley, CA: Basil Blackwell and Mott, Ltd., 1971), 71.

God for these very people, and that challenges in a stark and penetrating way any decision of a Christian people to declare war against another nation."[7]

On the thirtieth annual World Day of Prayer, Pope Francis met with leaders of the world's religions to pray, insisting that "God is the God of peace, there is no god of war: what creates war is evil, it is the devil, who wants to kill everyone." The Pope also suggested that all humanity should experience shame for warfare. "While we pray today, it would be good if each one of us should feel ashamed." Ashamed, he said, "that humans, our brothers, are capable of doing this."[8]

Can Christians be patriotic yet question using war to advance their own nation's interest? It is not a merely hypothetical question. Bishop Franz Joseph Rarkowski, Catholic Military Bishop for Germany during World War II, preached that German soldiers were obliged to serve both God and the Third Reich.[9] He encouraged good Christians to participate in evil, and Germany is still repenting. More questioning, not less, was called for. True patriots who renounced the evil of Nazism were rare. Franz Jägerstätter, a simple, devout Austrian farmer, was beheaded in 1943 for refusing on religious grounds to fight as part of the Nazi army. On October 26, 2007, he was beatified by the Catholic Church. Among the thou-

---

7.   Monika Hellwig, *The Eucharist and the Hunger of the World* (Lanham, MD: Sheed and Ward, 1992), 83.

8.   Morning meditation in the chapel of the Domus Sanctae Marthae, "The Disgrace of War," https://w2.vatican.va/content/francesco/en/ cotidie/2016/documents/papa-francesco-cotidie_20160920_the- disgrace-of-war.html.

9.   Guenter Lewy, *The Catholic Church and Nazi Germany* (Cambridge, MA: DeCapo Press, 2000), 238.

sands who attended were his widow and four daughters. In his own town, in his own day, however, he was all alone. "His example raises anew perennial questions around the competing demands of God and Caesar, including what obligations a Christian has as a citizen of a state, what constitutes legitimate authority, and what is the significance of individual conscience."[10] It is good news to hear that famed director Terrence Malick is currently working on a movie about the life of Jagerstatter. It is scheduled for release in 2019.[11]

The obligation to "render to Caesar the things that are Caesar's," does not remove the demands of conscience and the gospel. Christians can and do disagree in their response to such demands. This questioning is uncomfortable, but necessary. In the end, some will decide that a given military expedition is "just." Others will decide "not this one." Some have decided "not ever." Through it all, they are called to love one another—not just those with whom they agree.

I argue here neither for patriotism nor for pacifism. Neither do I presume to know the Lord's heart better than anyone else. *The Pastoral Constitution on the Church in the Modern World* of the Second Vatican Council reflects the attitude with which I hope to proceed. It states that frequently "and legitimately so," the faithful will disagree, but cautions each side not to confuse its proposed solutions with the gospel message. During disagreement, no

---

10.   Tom Roberts, "A Man for the World," *National Catholic Reporter* (November 9, 2007), http://natcath.org/NCR_Online/archives2/2007d/110907/110907a.htm.

11.   https://thefilmstage.com/news/terrence-malick-announces-next-film-radegund-based-on-the-life-of-franz-jagerstatter/

one should "appropriate the Church's authority for his [or her] opinion,"[12] but rather, try to have an honest discussion, and preserve charity.

N.T. Wright, the Anglican Bishop of Durham, England, states vividly our need to discuss issues calmly:

> Part of the difficulty is that people haven't learned how to argue properly. What they have learned to do is declaim. And if I just declaim and you just declaim, then we clash like two rhinoceroses. And then we retreat, slightly bruised, to our own happy hunting grounds where our own folk like hearing the snortings that we make (continuing with the rhinoceros image) until it's time to have another one of those clashes. I really don't enjoy that. I do enjoy serious dialogue and debate. There hasn't been enough of that really.[13]

I hope that honest and charitable discussion, without declamation or "snorting," may lead us to agreement. As G.K. Chesterton famously and aptly quipped, "The Christian ideal has not been tried and found wanting. It has been found difficult and left untried."[14]

---

12. "Pastoral Constitution on the Church in the Modern World," *The Basic Sixteen Documents of Vatican II*, ed. Austin Flannery, O.P. (Northport, NY: Costello Publishing Company, 1996),#43.

13. N.T. Wright interview, http://www.hornes.org/theologia/travis-tamerius/interview-with-n-t-wright

14. G.K.Chesterton, "The Unfinished Temple," in *What's Wrong with the World* (New York: Mead and Co 1927), 48.

II

Prevailing Wisdom

"One reason that the church has become so bitterly divided over moral issues is that the community of faith has uncritically accepted the categories of popular US discourse about these topics, without subjecting them to sustained critical scrutiny in light of a close reading of the Bible."[15]

In 1956, my college educated and very religious brother was drafted into military service. During a routine training drill, the men were given rifles with bayonets, placed before a line of stuffed "dummies," and ordered to stab while shouting out the chant, "We are killers, we want blood." He couldn't make himself do it. He protested that he didn't want blood, that he had allowed himself to be drafted out of duty to his country, not out of a desire to kill. Perhaps because the drill sergeant didn't hear him, he didn't get into trouble. Eventually, he became an instructor in the cryptography school at Fort Gordon, a position that allowed him to fulfill his commitment and maintain a clear conscience. Although I was quite young when he told me about the incident, I still remember it clearly. Conscience was new territory for me then. I began to learn, however, that there are clear lines of distinction in the formation of

---

15. Richard B. Hays, *The Moral Vision of the New Testament* (San Francisco: Harper, 1996), 2.

conscience, and that firm moral principles should guide our actions.

Many Christians maintain an Old Testament viewpoint on the subject of violence and war.[16] "An eye for an eye and a tooth for a tooth" (Ex 21:24) seems a reasonable principle in the wake of traumas such as 9/11 or any of the atrocities perpetrated by terrorist groups like ISIS. A "theology" based on strict justice, returning wrong for wrong is appealing. Jesus, however, interprets that phrase in a different way. "You have heard that it was said, 'An eye for an eye and a tooth for a tooth.' But I say to you, Do not resist an evildoer. But if anyone strikes you on the right cheek, turn the other also....I say to you, Love your enemies and pray for those who persecute you (Mt 5:38-44).[17] According to Robert Tannehill, Jesus is not speaking literally. His words center on a "focal instance... in deliberate tension" with conventional life and thought. In other words, Jesus chooses to speak in a way that challenges how people normally live and think. He suggests the opposite of what we would naturally do. In this case, when hit, a person would tend to hit back. In his study of New Testament language, Tannehill notes that non-literal language often employs metaphor, which uses an extreme form to make a clear point. Metaphoric language leaves

16. Scholars generally find no place in the Jewish tradition for theological pacifism.
Bennett Muraskin, "Secular Jews and Pacifism," http://www.csjo.org/pages/essays/essaypacifismbennett.htm.
Michael Broyde, "Pacifism in Jewish Law," http://www.myjewishlearning.com/ideas_belief/warpeace/War_Peace_TO/War_Pacifism_Broyde.htm.

17. Robert C. Tannehill, "The Focal Instance as a form of New Testament Speech: A study of Matthew 5-39b-42," *Journal of Religion* 50 (1979): 379.

room for the uniqueness of complex situations. Hyperbole (e.g., "a log in the eye" [Jn 6:42]) refers to things which are obviously impossible; "turning the other cheek," however, "stands at the edge of the possible."[18] A nonviolent response to a strike on the cheek is possible.

The admonition to turn the other cheek is not intended simply as advice about responding to violence, but also as an example of the culture of honor and shame in the time of Christ. Further, as N.T. Wright has noted, "Turning the other cheek, going the second mile, and so forth, were not a summons to "be a doormat for Jesus," but were, themselves, a call to [non-violent] resistance, not just non-violence."[19] French scholar Rene Girard suggests the efficacy of Wright's interpretation: "If all mankind offered the other cheek, no cheek would be struck."[20]

Many have attempted to explain away Jesus' revisionist and subversive statements. "Dispensationalists say that the Sermon on the Mount is meant only for the millennium; Lutherans argue that it applies only in personal relation-

---

18. Ibid.
19. N.T. Wright, "Doing Justice to Jesus," http://www.ntwrightpage.com/ Wright_Justice_Jesus.htm. Originally published in *Scottish Journal of Theology* 50.3 (1997: 359–79).
20. Rene Girard, *The Girard Reader*, James G. Williams, ed., (New York: Crossroads, 1996), 184. Girard is a pioneer in understanding the formation of nonviolent human community. His foundational theories concern humans as mimetic, imitational creatures prone to rivalry and conflict which leads to violence, and the scapegoating mechanism by which violence is released through convergence on a victim. To him, violence is a byproduct of mimetic rivalry. A convert to Christianity, Girard sees that the "Spirit Paraclete stands with the innocent victim and is revealed through him." In *Violence Unveiled: Humanity at the Crossroads* (New York: Crossroads, 1995), 4, Gil Bailie says, "Girard has made the most sweeping and significant intellectual breakthrough of the modern age.

ships; Niebuhrians place it on a pedestal of irrelevance by honoring it as an impossible ideal."[21] But might not the Sermon on the Mount represent what Jesus actually thinks? He seemed to enjoy turning the Old Testament upside down.[22] Miroslav Volf, a Presbyterian who teaches at the Yale School of Divinity, grounds his theology in his experience of war in the Balkans. In struggling with questions about warfare, he has concluded that for most Christians, "We may believe in Jesus, but we do not believe in his ideas, at least not in his ideas about violence, truth, and justice....We are not quite prepared to take up our cross and follow the nonviolent Jesus."[23]

Some deflect these stark statements of Jesus by pointing out passages like Matthew 10:34-35: "Do not think that I have come to bring peace to the earth; I have not come to bring peace, but a sword." Scripture scholars understand that in this statement, "sword" is a metaphor for how the truth of Jesus divides and polarizes people. The metaphorical sword, in this case, is held by our enemies, often family members, but not by the disciples, who are

---

21. Ronald J. Sider, "A Call for Evangelical Nonviolence," *Christian Century* (September 15, 1976): 755.

22. N.T. Wright, *Jesus and the Victory of God* (Minneapolis: Fortress, 1996), 564-565: "He [Jesus] tells stories that subvert a typical Jewish reading of the way things are and ought to be. He marginalizes the all-important Jewish symbols of temple, land, family and Torah...He would be the means of the kingdom's coming, both in that he would embody in himself the renewed Israel and in that he would defeat evil once for all. But the way in which he would defeat evil would be the way consistent with the deeply subversive nature of his own kingdom-announcement... the way of the cross...He took upon himself the fate of the nation.... Politically, he modeled the program of peace and rejected the path of nationalistic resistance to Rome."

23. Miroslav Volf, *Exclusion and Embrace* (Nashville, TN: Abingdon Press, 1996), 276.

hated because of His name (see Lk 21:17), and "marked out as undesirables."[24]

Joachim Jeremias has noted interpretations of the Sermon on the Mount that are only partially accurate. For example, some commentators suggest that it presents ethical perfectionism, or an impossible ideal, or an interim ethic before the end of all things. Such interpretations miss the mark, he says, because the real purpose of these collected sayings of Jesus is to express the knowledge of the presence of salvation. They are not intended to point out the need for human effort or to express anxiety in the face of catastrophe, but that the salvation of God is here. For this reason, Jeremias adds, in the Gospel of Matthew, the Sermon on the Mount is followed by a collection of miracle stories. The evangelist wants to show that Jesus is messiah in word and deed, the one in whom the Spirit of God is manifested in its fullness.[25] Readers must remember, Jeremias says, that the Sermon on the Mount was designed for Jewish Christians. That is its *Sitz im Leben*, the setting or purpose of this teaching.[26] Before the teaching, there were to be the proclamation of the gospel, conversion, the overpowering reality of the good news. When the newly converted heard these sayings, therefore, they realized such words represented not an impossible ideal, but the reality that their sins had been forgiven, that they had found the pearl of great price, that they already belonged to the new creation. The "new aeon of God" had begun; in God's

---

24. Tom Wright, *Luke for Everyone* (London: Society for Promoting Christian Knowledge, 2001), 252.

25. Joachim Jeremias, *The Sermon on the Mount* (University of London: The Athlone Press, 1961), 8-17.

26. Jeremias, 23.

time and place, this is what life is like.[27] Therefore, Jesus teaches in "the imperative, the will of God...in all its earnestness."[28] He makes demands because "the light of the city of God cannot be hid, it shines in the world."[29] The Sermon on the Mount is not about ethics or morality, but about lived faith.

Some claim that generalizing from the words of Jesus, which refer to specific situations, people, and points in time, is anachronistic, misleading, or even simplistic. Perhaps such claims are correct. Certainly, scripture is not meant to be an ethical handbook or a mere series of behavioral guidelines. Yet as N.T. Wright notes, the life of heaven, the realm where God is already king, is the life originally intended for the world. "And those who follow Jesus are to begin to live by this rule here and now. That's the point of the Sermon on the Mount...to live in the present in the way that will make sense in God's promised future...arrived...in Jesus of Nazareth."[30] If the admonitions in the Sermon on the Mount apply not only to the behavior of individuals but to more generalized conduct, may nations justly defend themselves? If nations do have the right to self-defense, may Christians take part in it?

Some juxtapose Jesus' radical call to love of enemies and non-violent resistance and Paul's call in Romans 13 to obey authority. "Do you wish to have no fear of the authority? Then do what is good, and you will receive its

---

27. Ibid., 29.
28. Ibid., 31.
29. Ibid., 32.
30. Tom Wright, *Matthew for Everyone, Part One* (London: Society for Promoting Christian Knowledge: 2002), 38. (In his pastoral books, N.T. Wright uses the name Tom Wright.)

approval; for it is God's servant for your good. But if you do what is wrong, you should be afraid, for the authority does not bear the sword in vain! It is the servant of God to execute wrath on the wrongdoer" (Rom 13:3-6). This passage, however, must be read in context. The first fifteen chapters of Romans constitute a single literary unit. The passage about authority must be read in the context of the "mercies" of a loving God. Believers must never pay back evil for evil. They must bless those who persecute them and never take revenge, leaving judgment to God. Because God may order the powers of government does not mean that everything they do receives divine approval. Some interpret this text to mean that governments come into being by a specific providential act of God, and so deserves allegiance. History shows, as in the cruel governments of ancient Rome, of Adolf Hitler, or of Saddam Hussein, that even if legitimate, Christians were not called to obey them without question.

The virtue of patriotism includes social responsibility and citizenship. Patriotism differs from mere nationalism. That statement is said easily enough, but in actual circumstances the difference becomes less clear, as with those who serve in the military. In every nation, brave men and women have fought and died for freedom. One of the noblest men I know, a hero, served during the Vietnam War. He was the last American officer to board a helicopter evacuating from Cambodia local citizens who had worked for the United States. Despite incoming fire, he remained outside the aircraft, risking his own life until the last of the Cambodians had boarded. Having helped the Americans, they would have been killed had they remained.

Senator Jim Webb of Virginia, a former Marine, writes: "When you have personalized death, looked into the eyes of innocent people as the life drained out of them...when you have watched an enemy fight with ferocity and often with honor, you tend to conclude that on some level you have more in common with those you were trying to kill than you do with people who view wars only as an intellectual debate."[31] Soldiers who have faced the reality of war realize that it is not a matter of abstract reasoning.

Most are drawn to military service because they believe it to be their patriotic duty, even God's will and purpose for their lives. Scripture itself is ambiguous on the subject of warfare, as is church teaching. One cannot help but admire the sacrifices they make because they believe they are defending freedom itself. Their bravery is real and they do what they do with a clear conscience. In fact, the *Catechism of the Catholic Church* notes that "Those who are sworn to serve their country in the armed forces are servants of the security and freedom of nations. If they carry out their duty honorably, they truly contribute to the common good of the nation and the maintenance of peace."[32] Protecting the lives of others is, according to the Catechism, their "grave duty."[33]

Nevertheless, an individual must still follow his or her conscience. Those who have a change of heart or of conscience after signing up for military duty face a moral and legal quandary. The Church recognizes both absolute and situational pacifism, where an individual determines that he or she may not contribute to a specific military

31.   Jim Webb, *A Time to Fight* (New York: Broadway Books, 2008), cited in "What it Means to be a Leader," *Parade Magazine, South Bend Tribune.* (May 8, 2008): 4-5.

32.   *Catechism of the Catholic Church, Second Edition* (Washington, D.C: United States Catholic Conference, 1994), #2310, 556.

33.   *Catechism* #2321,558.

engagement because it contradicts Christian principles. The law and the military, however, do not. A soldier can receive a release from service because of a conversion to total pacifism as a conscientious objector, but not because of an opinion about a specific war. Understandably, the military could not function if soldiers could opt out at will; but it is increasingly argued[34] that Christians should not join the military at all, lest they be put in situations that violate their conscience, as it happened for many soldiers in Vietnam or in Iraq. Daniel Baker, of the Catholic Peace Fellowship, became a conscientious objector while in the military. He believes the chaplaincy itself is compromised. "As an enlisted soldier, I found it nearly impossible to talk with my chaplain as a representative of Christ and the church ('Father') rather than as someone who had military authority over me ('Sir'). I suspect that there are scores of soldiers who will not come forward because they do not feel free to open up their consciences to someone who is of equal rank to their commanding officer."[35]

Leyton Richards, an early 20th century British Congregationalist minister, has described the splendid virtues that flourish during war. Individuals exhibit heroism, self-sacrifice, a spirit of service, camaraderie, and much else. He cautions, however, "War could not be conducted in terms of its virtues alone, or it would cease to be war."[36] Some military figures have made even stronger critiques.

---

34. Gordon C. Zahn, "The Draft: An Occasion of Sin?" *America Magazine*. (August 9, 1980).

35. Daniel Baker, "Letter to the Editor," *America Magazine* (December 22, 2008).

36. Leyton Richards, *Christian Pacifism After Two World Wars: A Critical and Constructive Approach to the Problems of World Peace* (London: Independent Press, 1948).

According to historian Doris Kearns Goodwin, Edwin Stanton, Lincoln's secretary of war, a Quaker, found the strain of war unbearable. As a young man he had written, "Why it is that military generals are 'praised and honored instead of being punished as malefactors?' After all, the work of war is the making of widows and orphans—the plundering of towns and villages—the exterminating and spoiling of all, making the earth a slaughterhouse."[37]

Christians who sincerely believe that in certain circumstances they must participate in war deserve respect for their courage, decisiveness, and virtue. For them, to do less would be cowardly. It is reasonable to make such decisions. As Richard Hays notes, however, appealing to reason alone allows figures like Osama Bin Laden to label Americans as "Crusaders." Interrogating reason in the light of the gospel may be uncomfortable, but it is beneficial. As Hays notes, reason must "be healed and taught by Scripture, and our experience must be transformed by the renewing of our minds in conformity with the mind of Christ."[38] As noble as individual soldiers undoubtedly are, in contemporary circumstances being a serious Christian and waging war may be irreconcilable. Miroslav Volf writes, "If one decides to put on soldier's gear instead of carrying one's cross, one should not seek legitimation in the religion that worships the crucified Messiah. For there, the blessing is given not to the violent, but to the meek (Mt 5:5)."[39]

---

37. Doris Kearns Goodwin, *Team of Rivals. The Political Genius of Abraham Lincoln* (New York: Simon and Schuster, 2006), 562.

38. Richard B. Hays, The Moral Vision of the New Testament: Community, Cross, New Creation, A Contemporary Introduction to New Testament Ethics (New York: Harper Collins, 1996), 343.

39. Volf, 306.

Although historians disagree on the significance of this historical fact, Christians are not mentioned as serving in the military until the second century (170-180).[40] Reformation scholar Roland Bainton finds that the only exception seems to have been those serving outside combat, and only if the Christian was not forced to engage in the idolatry that the Roman military often required.[41] In the early Church, the role of a Christian in the military was understood in terms of the message of peace central to what Jesus taught and lived.

"The Lord, by taking away Peter's sword, disarmed every soldier thereafter," writes Tertullian.[42] Some conclude that the swords in this encounter show that Jesus armed his followers in anticipation of trouble. Noted scripture scholar Fr. Raymond Brown disagrees with such an interpretation.[43] He considers Peter's assault on the servant a misunderstanding of what a disciple should do, an action consistent with the disciples' failure to act properly throughout the Mount of Olives scene.[44] Others point out that at the Last Supper Jesus told the twelve,

---

40. David William Kling, *The Bible in History: How the Texts Have Shaped the Times* (London: Oxford University Press, 2004), 176. Jonathan Reiley-Smith disagrees with Kling's interpretation. In an interview in *Christianity Today* ("Holy Violence Then and Now: A historian looks at the causes and lingering effects of Christian warfare" [October 1, 1993] http://www.ctlibrary.com/3995), Reiley-Smith maintains that the lack solid of evidence indicates either that Christians did not serve or that they did serve, but their presence was taken for granted.

41. Roland H Bainton, *Christian Attitudes Toward War and Peace* (New York: Abington Press,1960), 299.

42. Tertullian, "On Idolatry," *Ante-Nicene Fathers*, Alexander Roberts, ed. (Grand Rapids, MI: Eerdman,1965), 3:73.

43. Raymond Brown, *Death of the Messiah, Volume 1* (New York: Doubleday, 1994), 689.

44. Brown,267.

"And the one who has no sword must sell his cloak and buy one" (Lk 22: 36). When they responded, "Lord, look, here are two swords," Jesus responded, "It is enough" (Lk 22:38). Brown points out that the passage does not demonstrate that everyone should have a sword, but that "Everyone should be prepared....Purse, bag, and sword are quasi-symbolic ways of concretizing necessary readiness."[45] "The response of the disciples that they have in their possession two swords shows that they have (mis)understood literally."[46] In Matthew, Jesus commands, "Put your sword back into its place," and continues "for all who take the sword, will perish by the sword" (Mt 26:52). "That sentiment is harmonious with Matthew 5:39, where Jesus forbids his followers to answer violent action by violent action, and with 10:39 which encourages them to be willing to lose their lives for his sake."[47] Brown also explains that the statement about perishing by the sword is a warning to all of Jesus' followers. Moreover, after reprimanding Peter for using his sword, Jesus touches the ear of the servant and heals him.

Before Constantine (280-337), no Christian writer approved of Christian participation in warfare.[48] The early Fathers of the Church were convinced Isaiah's prophecy about the coming of the Messiah (see Is 2) had been fulfilled. Not only had the word of the Lord gone forth from Jerusalem, but "the eschatological state of nonviolence and peace prophesied by Isaiah, had already

---

45. Ibid.,270.
46. Ibid.
47. Ibid., 276.
48. Roland H. Bainton, *Early Christianity* (New York: Van Nostrand, 1960), 52-55.

become reality in the church."[49] German scripture scholar
Fr. Gerhard Lohfink insists that the early Church's belief
that Isaiah had been fulfilled is essential, because "the Jews
argue quite correctly that if nothing in the world has been
changed, the Messiah cannot have come."[50] If, however,
the Messiah has come, then the prophecy of peace in
Isaiah 2 should have become reality. If not, it could be
argued, Jesus was not the Messiah. This "Jewish objection," Lohfink maintains, must be taken seriously. The
reply of the early Church to this objection was not "that
the world need not be changed, since redemption takes
place invisibly; nor is it that redemption will not occur
until the end of the world."[51] Rather, the Church answered
that the Messiah had come and that, in fact, the world
has changed. It has been transformed into the Messiah's
people who live according to the law of Christ. They go
through the world proclaiming "Peace to this house" (Lk
10:5). They prefer to be struck on the other cheek than to
retaliate (Matthew 5:39). The early Fathers insisted that
the new worship of God, the new manner of life, the new
creation, already had visible and tangible effects. Isaiah 2:4
had been fulfilled in the age of the Church, called to be a
sign of this new "aeon" that had come.[52] In the early days,
Lohfink adds, the Church grew rapidly because it was such
a believable, radiant sign of this new epoch.

With the Edict of Milan (313), Constantine mandated
toleration for all religions. This imperial pronouncement
ended the waves of persecution, but raised a new issue—

---

49. Gerhard Lohfink, *Jesus and Community* (Philadelphia, Fortress Press,
     1984), 173.
50. Lohfink, 175.
51. Ibid., 175.
52. Ibid., 175-178.

how to remain a Christian when the state required force to combat evil. In addition, the new popular status of Christianity diluted the faith. After 391, when Theodosius I ended state support for traditional Roman religion, Christianity conformed itself bit by bit to the ways of the world. In the late 4th century, Basil of Caesarea noted that killing in war was permitted under some circumstances, but as penance the killer had to "abstain from communion for three years."[53] The early Church had an uneasy time coming to accept as "fact" that Christians could kill.

Under Constantine, many Christians begin to think that since the emperor was also Christian, they should fight in Rome's defense. A generation later this change compelled the great theologian, Augustine, to address the relationship between Christians and warfare. He did so by turning towards the Old Testament. Roland Bainton considers Augustine's position crucial because "It continues to this day in all essentials to be the ethic of the Roman Catholic Church and of the major Protestant bodies."[54]

It would seem logical for Augustine to begin with the Old Testament, as it is filled with war on behalf of God. God himself is called a warrior. Surely, some would say, the Old Testament makes a "case" for war and is "proof" that God sanctions it. Although that assertion may be disputed, the Old Testament's witness concerning war cannot. Some don't even attempt to reconcile the Old and New Testament "versions of God." Marcion (85-160) went so far as to sever the two completely. His dualist theology held that there were two gods, the one who created the world

---

53. Louis J. Swift, *The Early Fathers on War and Military Service* (Wilmington, DE: Michael Glazier, 1983), 94.

54. Bainton, *Christian Attitudes Towards War and Peace*, 99.

and the one who was revealed by Jesus. Jesus, he believed, was not the Messiah predicted in the Old Testament but the son of the good God sent to redeem humans from bondage. Marcion was declared a heretic, yet his dualism still surfaces in references to the "Old Testament God of Wrath" and the "New Testament God of Love."

Unlike Marcion, Augustine accepted the Old Testament and found it easy to reconcile with the New Testament. His arguments concerning warfare, therefore, are based on his understanding of the obligations of love. He argued that Christian rulers had an obligation to make peace for the protection of their subjects even if a threat could be eliminated only through force of arms. Five centuries later, St. Thomas Aquinas also placed the morality of warfare into the context of love, defining three necessary conditions for war: legitimate authority, just cause, and right intention.

At its basis, just war theory holds that a war must be declared for a "just cause," entered into with a "right intention," waged by a "legitimate authority," have a "reasonable chance of success," show that the good would outweigh the harm [proportionality], be used as a "last resort," and lend itself to "comparative justice" (the harm inflicted being less than that done by the enemy). If, these restrictions having been considered, war is still declared, the theory further delineates the behavior of those who wage war. They must discriminate between combatants and noncombatants and must use only force that is comparable to the harm received.[55]

---

55.   John A McHugh, O.P. and Charles J. Callan, O.P., *Moral Theology on War* (New York: Joseph F. Wagner, Inc, 1958).

In the *City of God,* Augustine aimed to convince a pagan audience that their values were "hollow realities" compared to the "supreme good," which is the goal of Christian striving (19:4). To illustrate this, he makes several observations about warfare. First, he comments on the "wretchedness" of social obligations that compel citizens to choose between lesser and greater evils. Given this unavoidable conflict, the truly wise person will

> Lament the fact that he is faced with the neces-sity of waging just wars of defense from the greater injustice of an aggressor. No wise person will cheer even a defensive war with any degree of patriotic exuberance; to contemplate warfare "without heartfelt grief" only shows that one "has lost all human feeling."[56]

Although his letter to Boniface speaks of the obligation of military action as an obligation of love to the neighbor,[57] Augustine called for soldiers who killed in war to perform three years of penance.

Most judgments concerning Christians and warfare are based on Augustine's (and Ambrose's) "just war theory," which maintains that under the right conditions violence may, in fact, be virtuous; there are good wars and bad wars. Some believe, however, that by justifying state violence, the Church relinquished its theology of peace as recon-ciliation with God the Creator.[58] Those who advocate this

---

56. Augustine, *City of God,* David Knowles, ed. (Baltimore, MD: Penguin Books, 1972), 19:7, 862.

57. Oliver O'Donovan, *The Just War Revisited* (London: Cambridge University Press,2003), 9.

58. Reed Anthony Carlson, "What Is It Good For? Nonviolence In A Violent

theological just war principle believe that "In the face of an injustice that is ongoing...it is in keeping with love of neighbor for the Christian to intervene on the neighbor's behalf in order to free the neighbor from this harm."[59] When that neighbor is not an individual, but a country, further principles determine whether war is justified. From Augustine onward, all scholars who support one or another of the just war theories consider warfare only as a last resort to protect innocent lives, something usually best left to peaceful means.

Since the time of Augustine, disagreement has continued between those who hold with "just wars of defense" and those who find all war incompatible with Christianity. Contemporary scholar Richard Hays, for example, disagrees with Augustine's position. "In fact, Mathew 26:51-52 [in the garden of Gethsemane, when Jesus told Peter to put his sword away] serves as an explicit refutation of this idea. There is no foundation whatever in the Gospel of Mathew for the notion that violence in defense of a third party is justifiable."[60] Nevertheless, most would concur that "love can sometimes smite, and even slay."[61]

Because its principles are widely ignored, some argue that just war theory as it has been articulated is outdated.

World: Part V," 19 January 2009, http://theophiliacs.com/2009/01/19/what-is-it-good-for-nonviolence-in-a-violent-world-part-v/.

59. Presbytery of Greater Atlanta. *A Call for Conversation: Non-violence and Abolition of War*. Part 1 is written by Victor McCracken. Albert Curry Winn, a retired Presbyterian minister who has served as moderator of the 119th PCUS General Assembly (1979), wrote its summary of the pacifist tradition. http://www.presbyteryofgreateratl.org/ministry_teams/outreach/peacemaking/alternativepaper-Maydraft.htm.

60. Hays, 324.

61. O'Donovan, 9.

Gerard Powers, director of policy studies at the University of Notre Dame's Joan B. Kroc Institute for International Peace Studies, argues that because modern warfare is so destructive, the primary criterion for resorting to war can only be securing a just peace. In an era of terrorism, Powers maintains, moral obligations must be upheld. Rather than discard the just war tradition because it is sometimes misunderstood or misused, he proposes an insistence upon "a strict or narrow interpretation of just war norms. According to a narrow or strict interpretation of just war norms....resort[ing] to nuclear war is morally impermissible."[62] Further, he notes, "The experience of total war in the 20th century, the threat of a nuclear holocaust, and the fact that civilians have increasingly been the main victims of war, have led the Church to be very skeptical about the ability of modern war to meet just war criteria. Skepticism, however, does not mean rejection."[63] It was, he points out, the "refinement and narrowing of the just war tradition, not the embrace of pacifism, which ultimately delegitimized holy war within mainstream Christianity."[64] The churches' "deligitimation" of war that Powers speaks of can be seen in the recent condemnation by both Catholic and mainline Protestant leaders of the IRA and Loyalist paramilitary violence in Northern Ireland as a violation of just war principles.

Although just war theory remains controversial, many who work in international relations consider some version of it essential for settling future disputes. To this end, the Global Ethics and Religion Forum, a non profit group

---

62. Gerard Powers. Private correspondence, [November 1, 2008]
63. Gerard Powers, "Catholic Peacebuilding: Moving Beyond Just War vs. Pacifism," *Prism* 20 (Winter 2008): 14.
64. Powers, 15.

dedicated to increasing global ethical responsibility, has formed a study group to revise just war theory for the 21st century. These sixty scholars, a multi-cultural group with representatives of every major religion, hold yearly conferences in Southern California and at Cambridge University. They have produced films such as *The Sacred Planet, Patterns for Peace: India as a Model for Peace in a Multi-Religious Society,* and *Global Voices for Human Rights.*

The *Catechism of the Catholic Church* reaffirms just war theory,[65] but the experience of war in the nuclear age—from Hiroshima to Baghdad—suggests that it needs to be rethought. Who decides whether the cause is just? Where is the comparative justice? Modern weapons, no matter how carefully used, cause "dis-proportionate" death and destruction. The more than 100 million land mines that have been sown,[66] remain long after hostilities have ceased. If non-nuclear weapons cause such extensive harm, consider the lack of proportion in nuclear warfare. At least twenty nations have, or are attempting to get, nuclear weapons. By some estimates, at least 23,000 are deployed.[67] With "means" such as these, can any war be justified?

Although the Catholic Church maintains its position on just war, it has begun to consider the unrestrained deadliness of modern warfare. Calling the arms race one of the greatest "curses" on the human race, Vatican II stated that "Providence urgently demands of us that we free ourselves from the age-old slavery of war."[68] Pope John XXIII's 1963

---

65.   #2309, 556.
66.   Sider.
67.   Ibid.
68.   "Pastoral Constitution on the Church in the Modern World," 81.

encyclical, *Pacem in terris*, finds just war in the nuclear age "barely imaginable," and that "it no longer makes sense to maintain that war is a fit instrument with which to repair the violation of justice."[69] In his 1965 address to the United Nations General Assembly, Pope Paul VI famously pleaded, "War no more." The popes since have continued the same exhortation.

During the 1991 Persian Gulf War, Cardinal Josef Ratzinger articulated Pope John Paul II's clear opposition: "The Pope expressed his thought with great clarity [that] there were not sufficient reasons to unleash a war."[70] As events were building up to the invasion of Iraq, John Paul II, described a potential war there as a "defeat for humanity."[71] Only peace, he said, would lead to a more just and caring society because "Violence and arms can never solve human problems."[72] Months before the 2002 invasion, Cardinal Ratzinger, now Pope Benedict XVI, said of the war that it "seems to me...that the damage would be greater than the values one hopes to save."[73]

---

69. Pope John XXIII, *Pacem in Terris* 127. Quoted in Lisa Sowle Cahill, *Love Your Enemies: Discipleship, Pacifism and Just War Theory* (Minneapolis, MN: Augsburg Fortress,1989), 98.

70. David Oderberg, "Teaching Tradition," *National Review Online* (May 2005), http://www.nationalreview.com/articles/214336/teaching-tradition/david-s-oderberg. In this article Oderberg clearly disagrees with Pope John Paul II, commenting that on Iraq, the pope was wrong and George Bush was right.

71. Pope John Paul II, to the Vatican diplomatic corps, January 13, 2003. Quoted in Frank Bruni, "Threats and Responses. The Vatican; Pope Voices Opposition, His Strongest, To Iraq War: January 14, 2003," *New York Times* (May 20, 2003), 12.

72. Pope John Paul II, Address to members of the Italian religious television channel *Telespace*, March 22, 2003.

73. Cardinal Josef Ratzinger, http://foro.univision.com/univision/board/message?board.id=politicaeneeuu&message.id=48631.

The Bishops' Conferences of Canada, Germany, England, Ireland, Wales, Scotland and France also discouraged that war. Again, at a press conference on May 2, 2003, Pope Benedict XVI suggested that "given the new weapons that make possible destructions that go beyond the combatant groups, today we should be asking ourselves if it is still licit to admit the very existence of a 'just war.'"[74]

Pope Francis has taken this question to a new level, proposing to develop a clearer understanding of all the teachings of the New Testament but under contemporary realities. He asks "What would Jesus do?" As Graham E. Fuller has noted, "This phrase is not as superficial as it seems. It poses a serious challenge to Christians (and not just Christians) to consider how the moral teachings of Jesus might be made relevant to today's world. Not as airy-fairy sentimental idealism but as practical and meaningful muscular morality." The comments by Pope Francis came in the context of the landmark Nonviolence and Just Peace conference organized in Rome in April 2016 by the Vatican's Pontifical Council for Justice and Peace. The conference urged the church to integrate Jesus' nonviolence throughout the life of the church and to "no longer use or teach the just war theory."[75]

The Church's role consists in enunciating clearly the principles, in forming the consciences of men and in insisting on the moral exercise of just war. While no papal statement has officially reversed the Church's teaching on just war, the popes have deemed no recent war just. Yet, as

---

74. "The Moral Compass of Benedict XVI: Where Will His Commitment to Peace Lead Us?" *The Sign of Peace* 5.1. (Spring 2006), 17.

75. Graham E. Fuller, "Pope Francis Takes On 'Just War' Theory" (April 14, 2016), https://consortiumnews.com/2016/04/14/pope-francis-takes-on-just-war-theory/.

with other aspects of modern life, many of the faithful pay such guidance little or no heed.

The teaching of the Church concerning nuclear weapons is particularly striking. The Second Vatican Council denounced only one human behavior. *The Pastoral Constitution on the Church in the Modern World* states, "Any act of war aimed indiscriminately at the destruction of entire cities or of extensive areas along with their population is a crime against God and man himself. It merits unequivocal and unhesitating condemnation."[76] The United States Council of Catholic Bishops has withdrawn the limited acceptance for nuclear weapons it expressed during the Cold War. In their 1983 *Pastoral Letter on War and Peace* the bishops stated:

> Under no circumstances may nuclear weapons or other instruments of mass slaughter be used for the purpose of destroying population centers or other predominantly civilian targets. Retaliatory action...must also be condemned....We do not perceive any situation in which the deliberate initiation of nuclear war, on however restricted a scale, can be morally justified....We need a "moral about-face." The whole world must summon the moral courage and technical means to say no to nuclear conflict; no to weapons of mass destruction; no to an arms race which robs the poor and the vulnerable; and no to the moral danger of a nuclear age which places before humankind indefensible choices of constant terror or surrender.[77]

---

76. *Pastoral Constitution on the Church in the Modern World*, 80, 266-277.
77. National Conference of Catholic Bishops, "God's Promise and Our Response," in *A Pastoral Letter on War and Peace* (Washington, D.C.:

The hierarchy considers the abolition of nuclear weapons a precondition for peace. The popes have spoken out strongly against recent wars, though none have been nuclear. Lisa Cahill, professor of theology at Boston College, notes that since *Pacem in terris,* papal teaching has evolved beyond a "just war" theory that assesses justice only in relation to the common good.[78] In *The Just War Ethic,* Fr. J. Bryan Hehir, former Secretary of the Department of Social Development and World Peace of the United States Catholic Conference, notes that "current Catholic (papal) teaching is veering anomalously close to absolute pacifism."[79]

More recently, at a conference on nuclear disarmament hosted by the Vatican in 2017, Pope Francis indicated that deterrence itself is no longer acceptable. "The existence of nuclear weapons creates a false sense of security that holds international relations hostage and stifles peaceful coexistence. . . .The threat of their use as well as their very possession is to be firmly condemned."[80]

Cardinal Joseph Bernardin's sense that every human life has transcendent value "has led a whole stream of the Christian tradition to argue that life may never be taken. That position is held by an increasing number of Catholics."[81] Some have likened Bernardin's position to the "seamless garment" of Christ, using that image to represent a unified or consistent ethic, treating life as sacred

---

USCC/Office of Publishing and Promotion Services, May 3, 1983), 3-4.

78. Lisa Sowle Cahill, *Love Your Enemies: Discipleship, Pacifism, and Just War Theory* (Minneapolis, *MN:* Augsburg Fortress 1994), 211.

79. Quoted in Cahill, 33.

80. http://catholicherald.co.uk/news/2017/11 pope-francis-the-possession-of-nuclear-weapons-should-be-firmly-condemned/.

81. Joseph Cardinal Bernardin, "Cardinal Bernardin's Call for a Consistent Ethic of Life," *Origins* 13, 29 (December 29, 1983), 491-94.

from conception to death, ruling out abortion, euthanasia, capital punishment and killing in warfare.

Others religious leaders also speak this way. Presbyterian author Albert Curry Winn has written that the "bankruptcy" of just war theory is evident because it has seldom prevented wars, and because "Christian" nations always reason that their cause is just. He further notes that all modern technological warfare contradicts just war criteria. "Nuclear war would only make clear what has already happened to proportionality and discrimination at Coventry, Dresden, the firebombing of Tokyo, the destruction of Baghdad, and low intensity warfare in Central America."[82]

Christians seem to have accepted what theologian Walter Wink has called the "myth of redemptive violence"—that good ends can come from violent means, and that violence may even be necessary to solve problems and make peace. In discussions concerning modern warfare the Aristotelian ethical principle that "the end does not justify the means" has been twisted. This moral concept assumes that the end is good. If the "end" of an action is to kill, no means can ever be good. If the end is to secure justice, some means may be good and others evil. A corollary of this principle is that good ends can never be secured through evil means. In the question of war, is the only criterion success? If so, then does anything which contributes to success become justified? "Success may be the standard by which we measure the expediency of the means, but expediency is one thing and moral justification is another."[83]

---

82. Albert Curry Winn. *Ain't Gonna Sudy War No More: Biblical Ambiguity and the Abolition of War* (Louisville, KY: Westminster/Jon Knox Press, 1993),195.

83. Mortimer Adler. "Does the End Ever Justify the Means?" (February,

During the fourth and fifth centuries, views on warfare changed radically. As late as the eleventh century, all who shed blood in battle faced heavy penances and penalties. During the Crusades, instead of doing penance for shedding blood in battle, soldiers were urged to "expiate your sins by victories over the infidels."[84] Many who admire the Crusaders' "courage" in fighting to regain holy land and sites excuse their savagery by arguing that had Christians seized Muslim lands and holy sites, the Muslims would have fought similarly. This argument avoids the consideration that Christians, because they are followers of Christ, must hold themselves to a different moral standard. Christians have killed not only Muslims, but one another with equal ferocity. C. Wright Mills points out that "From the time of Constantine to the time of global radiation and the uninterceptible missile, Christians have killed Christians and have been blessed for doing so by other Christians."[85]

Prevailing wisdom has held that warfare, while repugnant and hideous, is necessary in an evil world. As part of that world, Christians have felt compelled to fight. That is the proposition to be considered next.

2001), http://www.cooperativeindividualism.org/adler_does_end_justify_means.html.

84.   Bernard of Clairvaux, "Letter Promoting the Second Crusade," in James Harvey Robinson, *Readings in European History, Vol. 1* (Boston: Ginn & Co., 1904),330-333.

85.   C. Wright Mills, *The Causes of World War Three*. (New York: Ballantine Books, 1960), 169.

III

The Case for War?

The greatest intracanonical challenge to the witness of the Sermon on the Mount concerning nonviolence and love of enemies comes not from any New Testament text, but from the Old Testament, particularly the holy war texts commanding Israel to kill its enemies.[86]

Many Christians support war, even when it means killing other Christians. In fact, most people do. A Quinnipiac University poll taken in 2017 noted that fully 46% of Republicans (many of whom are Christian) said they would support a preemptive strike against North Korea. Conservative theologians like George Weigel agree.[87]

In a strongly worded argument against such thinking about pre-emptive war, Mark Shea wrote in the *National Catholic Register*, "Pre-emptive war, being neither a response to an actual act of aggression nor a last resort is, itself, an act of aggression. It should be as morally desirable…as the thought of amputating one's own healthy leg because you fear that in five years you might step on a nail and get gangrene. . . .That is why the late Joaquin Navarro-Valls, speaking on behalf of Pope John Paul II said, "He who

---

86. Hays, 336.
87. "A Moral Question—Is It Ever Right to Go First?" *The Michigan Catholic* (11 January 2002): 6.

decides that all pacific means provided by the international law are exhausted, assumes a grave responsibility in front of God, in front of his own conscience and in front of history." Shea continues, "The argument that the silence of the Catechism on pre-emptive war is an argument in *favor* of it is like the argument that the silence of the Catechism on the subject of ritual cannibalism means that cooking and eating human beings in religious ceremonies is not "always wrong." Yes it is. And so is pre-emptive war."[88]

Some historians of the Crusades and some Christian theologians invoke St. Basil to justify war even if it is pre-emptive and will mean killing other Christians. Murder, they admit, was always condemned in the early Church. But some killing, such as in warfare is not murder. In the "First Canonical Epistle" (371), Basil writes, "Our fathers did not think killing in war was murder..." Nevertheless, he continues in the same sentence, "yet I think it advisable for such as have been guilty of it to forbear communion three years."[89]

Modern scholars of Hebrew have even argued that *ratsách* (Exodus 20:13) should be translated, "Thou shalt not murder," rather than "Thou shalt not kill." But Wilma Ann Bailey, professor of Hebrew and Aramaic at the Christian Theological Seminary in Indianapolis, Indiana, concludes that the Hebrew word *rtsh* does not signify "murder" at other places where it appears in scripture. She notes that the English word "murder" is a term used to make a legal distinction; moreover, the

---

88. http://www.ncregister.com/blog/mark-shea/pre-emptive-war-and-the-protestant-semi-permeable-membrane.

89. St. Basil the Great, in Phillip Schaff, et al. *Nicene and Post-Nicene Fathers: Series II, Volume XIV,* Canon 13, 605, http://en.wikisource.org/wiki/Nicene_and_Post-Nicene_Fathers:_Series_II).

Ten Commandments are general injunctions, not a list of particular and rare crimes.[90] Bailey points out that no American mainline translation used the term "murder" until the New Revised Standard Version in 1989, a change she ascribes to a melding of evangelicalism, patriotism, and militarism. Of all the major Christian traditions, she adds, only Roman Catholicism maintains the word "kill" in its version of the commandments.

Bailey emphasizes the significance of this choice, using this translation:

> Limiting the scope of the commandment to illegal one-on-one killing exempts the primary causes of unnatural deaths in the twentieth and early twenty first centuries: war, capital punishment, government policies of starvation or government sponsored terrorism, lack of health care and hygienic programs (clean water, clean air, absence of toxins in the environment), and preventable accidents and diseases that kill far more people.[91]

She believes its reverence for tradition motivates the Catholic Church to translate *rtsh* as "kill" rather than "murder." She notes that Catholicism considers itself not a religion of the book but a religion of the Word—the capital W signifying Christ. For Catholics, the Bible must be interpreted in light of his life and teaching. Further, she notes, the Catholic Church continues to base its vernacular translations on Jerome's Latin Vulgate, made from Greek and Hebrew sources. The word that his translation

---

90.   Wilma Ann Bailey, *"You Shall Not Kill" or "You Shall Not Murder"? The Assault on a Biblical Text* (Collegeville, MN: Liturgical Press, 2005), 24.

91.   Bailey, 80.

renders "kill" signifies wholesale slaughter, not just one-on-one violence.

Most Christians who accept that in some cases Christians may legitimately take human life do so because, like Niebuhr, they believe prohibiting killing altogether allows tyranny to proceed unchecked. Leyton Richards points out, however, that

> By a similar process of reasoning, Jesus was respon-
> sible for the tyranny of Rome and the destruction
> of Jerusalem; for he refused the invitation of the
> Zealots to wage a Messianic war, and he even
> counseled his compatriots to pay their dues to the
> tyrant who held Jerusalem in the grip of a military
> dictatorship.[92]

Other scholars, including Michael Gaddis (Syracuse), Darrell Cole (Drew), and John Helgeland (North Dakota State) reject the notion that the early Christians practiced nonviolence.[93] They argue that the apparent lack of evidence for Christians in the military before 170 CE suggests that few Roman soldiers converted, and that Christians were not allowed to join the legions even if they wanted to. Cole offers the particularly nuanced argument that according to Origen the early Christians did not oppose war itself, only their own taking part in it. They could

---

92.   Richards, 53
93.   See Michael Gaddis, *There is No Crime for Those Who Have Christ: Religion and Violence in the Christian Roman Empire* (Berkeley, CA: University of California Press, 2005); Darrell Cole, *When God Says War is Right. The Christian's Perspective on When and How to Fight.* (Colorado Springs, CO: Waterbrook Press, 2002); John Helgeland, "Christians and the Roman Army AD 173-337," *Church History* 43:2 (June, 1974):149-163,200.

participate, in Origen's view, only "spiritually," through prayer.

Some use Gnostic texts to justify their stance on killing. They take "The Gospel of Thomas" or various Apocryphal Acts to represent a popular Christian opinion that approved of violence. The Church did not include such texts in the canon for a reason. Helgeland points out that the apocryphal writings display strikingly different attitudes concerning violence than those held by the Church Fathers. In the apocryphal gospels, he notes, "Not a forgiving person, the youth Jesus carried grudges and left in his wake death and destruction. Parents of children in Nazareth came to Mary and Joseph complaining that Jesus was killing their children."[94] Because the Church rejected the Gnostic texts, the evidence they provide for what early Christians believed is unreliable.

Some would use canonical scriptures to justify killing, but the Bible should not be used as a handbook that specifies which behavior is ethical and which is not. Some cite the Old Testament's rules for warfare to justify Christian participation in war, but ignore its recommendation of capital punishment for cursing one's parents or breaking the Sabbath. How can one part of the Law be authoritative, but another not?[95] Read properly, as a whole, scripture unveils what God was doing at a particular time and place in human history. The Old Testament must be taken into account, even its stories of wars that the Chosen People

94. Andrew Holt, "Early Christian Views of War: A Bibliographic Essay" (Fall, 2006), http://www.crusades-encyclopedia.com/christianpacifism.html

95. Ralph Orr, "War in the Old Testament, http://www.wcg.org/lit/ethics/War02.htm.

celebrate because they believe God authorized or in some cases even commanded them to fight.

At the end of the story of creation in Genesis, the world is peaceful and orderly. Beginning with Chapter 3, however, it records the consequences of the Fall, including violence that affected beasts as well as humans. The Book of Exodus (17:10-13) contains the Bible's first mention of armies, and verses 14-17 portray Yahweh as a great warrior: "The Lord will have war with Amalek from generation to generation". In the Book of Deuteronomy (7:1-17), God commands Israel to "defeat them [the seven nations that were inhabiting the Promised Land], then you must utterly destroy them. Make no covenant with them and show them no mercy…: break down their altars, smash their pillars, hew down their sacred poles, and burn their idols with fire." The scriptures are filled with accounts of bloody war and rolling heads.

Genesis reveals the significance of creation. God brought something out of nothing; out of chaos, the Creator brought order, the harmony and wholeness of *shalom*. *Shalom* means much more than the absence of war. Biblical scholar Paul Hanson writes, "Perhaps the best way to begin to understand *shalom* is to recognize that it describes the realm where chaos is not allowed to enter, and where life can be fostered free from the fear of all which diminishes and destroys."[96] *Shalom* means more than the "mere" absence of war. "Yet…the definition of peace…dims our eyes to the fact that the absence of war remains one of the distinctive meanings of 'peace' and that there is nothing 'mere' about it."[97]

---

96. Paul Hanson, "War and Peace in the Hebrew Bible," *Interpretation* 38 (1984): 347.

97. Paul Valliere, *Holy War and Pentecostal Peace* (New York: The Seabury

The theme of *shalom* runs throughout the Old Testament. Despite story after story of war, destruction, and judgment, the Old Testament is about God's initial and ongoing desire for peace, harmony and restoration. That image of peace appears like a counterpoint to the theme of war, particularly in the prophets who proclaim the hope of a different world. Isaiah and Micah speak of a day when nations will beat swords into plowshares (Is 2:4; Mi 4:3), and where nation would not lift up sword against nation.

Isaiah and Micah might seem to be idealistic dreamers, but their vision speaks to a nuclear age. Because the chaos of nuclear war would wipe out *shalom*, Bruce Birch, a Methodist minister and scripture scholar, believes that "nuclear war must be the ultimate sin—representing the absolute triumph of chaos and the end of all possibility for wholeness and well-being."[98] Jeremiah, Birch says, speaks to the contemporary world. The prophet advised the exiles in Babylon to "seek the welfare of the city where I have sent you into exile, and pray to the Lord on its behalf, for in its welfare you will find your welfare." (Jer 29:7). The word translated as welfare is *shalom*. We cannot act out of wishful nostalgia for a world we would like to have, Birch adds; rather, "we must seek the *shalom* of the nuclear world we do have."[99]

Anabaptists and others like the Methodist theologian Richard Hays believe that Jesus resolves the Old Testament's "mixed message" concerning war. Jesus declares that in the

---

Press, 1983), 155.

98.   Bruce C Birch, "Old Testament Foundations for Peacemaking in the Nuclear Era," *The Christian Century* (December 4, 1985): 115.

99.   Birch, 119.

new reign of God, people will love their enemies. Just as the New Testament supersedes Old Testament requirements such as circumcision and dietary laws, so too, the explicit teaching and example of non-violence in the life of Jesus reshapes our "understanding of God and of the covenant community in such a way that killing enemies is no longer a justifiable option.[100]

But didn't Jesus curse fig trees, drive pigs off a cliff, take a whip to tables in the temple and lash out at the Scribes and Pharisees as a "brood of vipers"(Mt 23:33)? Didn't he even call Peter "Satan"? Such confrontational words and deeds should be considered as part of Jesus' role as a prophet. He did not invent the terminology, which was commonly used in prophecy. For example, Psalm 140 begins, "Deliver me, O Lord, from evildoers....They make their tongue sharp as a snake's, and under their lips is the venom of vipers." Even his act of turning over of the table in the temple demonstrated prophetic dramatic disruption, not destruction and assault.

Methodist theologian Rev. Dr. Gordon Wong has attempted to reconcile what seems to be the approval of war and violence in the Old Testament with New Testament nonviolence by examining Levi, the "thirteenth tribe." In the covenant with Levi, God promised life and peace. In turn, therefore, the Levites were forbidden to go to war and were commissioned to promote life and peace. This covenant, Wong believes "is to continue to the priesthood of Believers... Through Christ, the Church became a royal priesthood.... The Christian, just like the Levite is to have a ministry of life and peace."[101]

---

100. Hays, 336.
101. Gordon Wong, "Pacifism Or Peace?: War, Peace And Justice In The Old

A prophetic stream preceded Jesus, and he chose to continue in it. Wong cites Isaiah 65:25 ("The wolf and the lamb shall feed together, the lion shall eat straw like the ox; but the serpent—its food shall be dust! They shall not hurt or destroy on all my holy mountain, says the Lord."), and Zechariah 9:9-10, which describes a victorious king who rides not on a war horse but on a donkey, an ancient symbol of the desire to rule with gentleness and to promote peace. He also notes that the Old Testament recognizes human force not only to be dangerous, but possibly inherently defiling. "Numbers 31 expresses genuine ambivalence concerning the ethics of war. The cause is holy; the war is ritualized, but the killing defiles. Thus as one enters war ritually one must exit with separation, cleansing, and sacrifices of atonement."[102] The same ambivalence appears when God forbids David to build a temple because he had shed blood in battle. "You have shed much blood and have waged great wars; you shall not build a house to my name, because you have shed so much blood in my sight on the earth" (1 Chron 22:8). Wong suggests that the Old Testament "counsels neither war nor pacifism; it champions justice and peace."[103]

Presbyterian scholar Albert Curry Winn proposes that, although Jesus did not reconcile the ambiguity of the Old Testament, he did choose deliberately to continue in the prophetic stream that runs through the Hebrew Scriptures.

"From the great diversity of the Old Testament he chose the prophetic strain as that which is closest to the truth, as that in the light of which all the rest must be

---

Testament," *Church and Society* 5, no. 2: 64.

102. Wong, 64.

103. Ibid.

interpreted."[104] Jesus aligned himself as a prophet. He took the side of the marginalized, the lepers, the disabled, the grief stricken, widows, the poor, the orphan, the hungry, prostitutes, women, children.[105]

Winn notes that, in line with the prophets, Jesus predicted the destruction of Jerusalem because it had failed to read the signs of the times: "If you, even you, had only recognized on this day the things that make for peace!"(Lk 19:42).[106] Jesus wept at the city's imminent destruction because of its failure to recognize him: "They will crush you to the ground, you and your children within you, and they will not leave within you one stone upon another; because you did not recognize the time of your visitation from God" (Lk: 19:44). He steps beyond the prophets who preceded him by announcing that the "kingdom is already present.... in his ministry and the ministry of his followers.... (Mt 4:17, Lk 10:9) and that "the promised time of *shalom* is already at work in the world and will surely come!"[107]

The prophets were not idealistic dreamers. Spirit inspired, Jesus came to hold up before his people the vision and will of God. His food was to do the will of His Father, and as prophet, he restated and lived out his way and will of peace. According to Winn, in Jesus, "The ambiguity between the wrath and the love of God remains.... Perhaps it is part of the divine mystery, the divine abyss which human intelligence cannot plumb."[108] Vengeance is not yours, says the Lord, but mine. His wrath will fall on those

---

104. Winn, 129
105. Ibid., 132.
106. Ibid., 134.
107. Ibid., 139.
108. Ibid., 146.

who act unjustly. But "Jesus is very clear about how his followers are to behave. He does not encourage them to participate in the divine wrath....If they wish to be children of God, they are to love their enemies and pray for those who persecute them.(Mt 6:44-45)If they wish to be children of God they are to be peacemakers (Mt5:19)."[109]

Even in the Old Testament the wrath of God does not override the love that St. John says God "is." Consider, for example, Hosea 11:1-12. There, God seems truly angered at the faithlessness of his people, but even if Israel can reject its liberation and election by God, God cannot take back what he has offered. He says, "My heart recoils within me!" Or, as The Message Bible translates the passage, "I can't bear to even think such thoughts. My insides churn in protest." He will not act on his anger, because he is "God and not man." Although guilty, Israel is not sentenced, but freed. As the New Testament makes clear, God himself, in his Son, suffers the rejection, the punishment Israel deserved.

In his 2016 book *The Day the Revolution Began: Reconsidering the Meaning of Jesus's Crucifixion*, N.T. Wright argues against the stress on this view of the atonement, known often as penal substitution.

Wright is not saying that Penal Substitution is wrong. He is saying that the focus on Penal Substitution as the primary or only way to look at the atonement distorts our understanding of what Jesus did on the Cross.[110] The Father of Jesus is merciful. And yet mankind, as Rene Girard notes, because of the violence within it, often believes that

---

109. Winn, 146, 180. See also: 1 Pt 3:9; Mt. 5:11-12; Lk 6:22-23.

110. N.T. Wright, "God, 9/11, the Tsunami, and the New Problem of Evil," *Response* 28 (Summer 2005), http://www.spu.edu/depts/uc/response/summer2k5/features/evil.asp.

the "Father of Jesus is still a God of violence despite what Jesus explicitly says."[111] The relationship between the love and anger of God is clear. The Father's wrath is spent. The sword that hung over our heads has already pierced the side of Christ. The heart of God is love.

Winn argues that when the living, active memory of the apostolic Church faded, when church and state became one, when Augustine chose principles for examining the morality of warfare from the Old Testament, Jesus' deliberate choice to continue in the prophetic stream of scripture came to be misinterpreted. With Augustine's choice, Winn notes with some dismay, "The side of scriptural ambiguity that Jesus and the early church had rejected was now chosen afresh."[112] Gerrit Jan Heering states quite forcefully that in his opinion, Augustine reversed the will of the Lord. "This radical change in the Christian faith, in regard to so vital a matter as war, we cannot regard as other than a disastrous fall, as a fall into a condition which primitive Christianity would not have hesitated to call a condition of sin. We believe that history justifies our view."[113] Heering's work does betray a bias against the Catholic Church, and only God has the right to judge what is sin and what is not.

Nevertheless, it is possible that Christians may have strayed from the "way" of Jesus. Lohfink thinks so, and does not shy away from condemning contemporary moral decisions concerning war.

> That in 1914, Christians went enthusiastically to war against Christians, baptized against baptized,

---

111. Girard,186.

112. Winn, 194.

113. Gerrit Jan Heering, *The Fall of Christianity : A Study of Christianity, the State, and War* (New York: Garland, 1972), 35.

was not seen in any way as destruction of what the Church is in and of its very nature, a destruction that cried out to heaven, that was the real catastrophe. And that Hitler's war was a criminal act that Christians in Germany should have resisted from the outset was again not a question that disturbed the consciences of very many.[114]

Despite Lohfink's strong language, it is unlikely that many individuals, Christian or not, have ever been "enthusiastic" about going to war. Moreover, the history of World War II contains story after story of heroes whose consciences compelled them to resist Hitler and his policies, even so far as risking their own lives. What Lofink asserts here, however, reflects his own personal scandal at the horrors he witnessed as a child in Nazi Germany. "I saw men and women who were forced to sew a yellow star of David on their garments; then one day I didn't see them any more."[115]

Those in Germany who failed to resist Hitler's war may have acted as they did because they considered him a legitimate authority, or may even have been encouraged by some church leaders to fight for their country. Their failure to challenge prevailing wisdom could reoccur among Christians if they do not come to understand more deeply their true identity, and act accordingly.

---

114. Lohfink, *Does God Need the Church?*, 315.
115. Ibid.

IV

Christian Identity

*The mystery that has been hidden throughout the
ages and generations but has now been revealed to his
saints...is Christ in you, the hope of glory. (Col 1:26,27)*

Have nuclear and biological weapons rendered obso-
lete previously "moral" determinations of justice and proportionality in warfare? Does rationalization place nearly
insurmountable obstacles in the path of those who seek
the love that Christ has brought on earth, a love all are
called to live? Is it possible that "reasonable" responses to
violence do not conform to the mind of Christ?

The Sermon on the Mount suggests that evil will be
defeated "not by military victory, but by a *doubly* revolu-
tionary method: turning the other cheek, going the second
mile, the deeply subversive wisdom of taking up the cross.
The agenda which Jesus mapped out for his followers was
the agenda to which he himself was obedient."[116] Many
Christians find "turning the other cheek" unthinkable. As
Richard Hays notes, they consider it simply bad advice.
"Such action makes sense only if the God and Father of
Jesus Christ actually is the ultimate judge of the world...
Turning the other cheek makes sense if and only if all
authority in heaven and on earth has been given to Jesus."[117]

---

116. N.T. Wright, *Jesus and the Victory of God*, 465.
117. Hays, 338.

Since Jesus *does* have such authority, does faith then compel Christians to follow his advice and his example?

Christians may lose sight of the very nature of Jesus himself, but **their fundamental blind spot regards their own identity as Christians**. They don't see clearly who they are. They say they are followers of Christ, and that may be true. But Christians are more than followers.[118] They are, according to the scriptures, Christ himself in this world.

- "I have been crucified with Christ; and it is no longer I who live, but it is Christ who lives in me. And the life I now live in the flesh I live by faith in the Son of God, who loved me and gave himself for me." (Gal 2:19-20)

- "I am in my Father and you in me and I in you." (Jn 14:19-20)

- "Thus he has given us...his precious and very great promises, so that through them you...may become participants of the divine nature." (2 Pt 1:4)

The good news is that "... the effect of our sharing in the body and blood of Christ is to change us into what we receive. As we have died with him, and have been buried and raised to life with him, so we bear him within us, both in body and in spirit, in everything we do"(St. Leo the Great, Sermon LXIII, On the Passion, XII).

What Leo the Great says is most important. Christians are a Eucharistic people. When they share in the bread and wine at the table of the Lord's Supper, they are changed into what they receive. They become what they eat. The bread

---

118. William Spohn, *What are they saying about Scripture and Ethics?* (New York: Paulist Press, 1985),122. Spohn ties imitation of God, a key theme of the Sermon on the Mount, to participation in the life of God by the power of the Spirit.

of life that Christians consume forms Christ in them. They are not fed merely to get strength to do his work, though that is true; even more, they are fed to become his body in the world. Life in Christ is a response to the baptismal initiation by which Christians have entered into Christ's death and resurrection and have been adopted as sons and daughters of God. This is celebrated in every Eucharist. That is why Catholic Christians offer one another a sign of "peace" at the halfway point of every Mass, and are sent forth at the end with the words "Go in peace." Jesus is the place of reconciliation. This is his way. This is who Christians are called to be; many positions they take must be considered "as Christ, in Christ."

The Christ life of the sacraments and the peace of Christ share the same deep source. Michael Baxter, professor of Moral Theology and Christian Ethics at the University of Notre Dame puts it this way:

> The irreducibly social character of peace, in the Catholic theological tradition, is illustrated in the great anti-Arian treatise *On the Incarnation,* where Athanasius declares that the truth of the divinity of Christ has been demonstrated in Egypt inasmuch as the spread of Christianity has brought that land peace, true peace, God's peace. If we were to inquire as to how this peace is established, the answer would have to be that it is through the lives of those claimed by Christ in baptism, confirmation, and Eucharist; lives that are so transformed that Christians may be described as "partakers of Christ" or, simply, as "Christs." [119]

---

119. Michael J. Baxter, "Just War and Pacifism: A 'Pacifist' Perspective in Seven Points," *Houston Catholic Worker* 24 (May-June 2004), http://www.cjd.org/paper/baxpacif.html.

V

Contrast Society

"You are the salt of the earth." (Mt 5:13)

Salt provides zip to bland food. "But," the passage
from Matthew continues, "if salt has lost its taste…it is no
longer good for anything, but is thrown out and trampled
under foot." Christians without salt are useless to the mission of Christ. Individually and communally, their witness
and way of life needs to stand in contrast with the larger
culture. They must be the "sign of contradiction" (Lk
2:34, Acts 28:22). Scripture scholars Gerhard and Norbert
Lohfink formulated the notion of a "contrast society." In
their covenant with God, who is the God of all nations, the
people of Israel serve two functions. They are mediators of
the relationship between the Creator and all other nations,
as well as models of a community that lives out divine
righteousness in concrete ways. They become a new kind
of family, a "light to the nations."[120] Although some think
the Lohfinks' model has encouraged sectarianism,[121] most
believe that it sheds light on the Church's life and mission to "nurture, nourish, and evoke a consciousness and
perception alternative to the consciousness and perception

---

120. Hamm, 33.
121. David Balch, "Review of Lohfink's *Jesus and Community*," *Journal of
Biblical Literature* 106 (December,1987): 715-717.

of the dominant culture around us."[122] Cahill argues that
such Christian witness does not imply sectarianism, but "a
hope for social change through example and education."[123]
It is right and good and just for Christians to engage the
culture around them. They should support and encourage
all that is good in society, in culture, art, literature, music,
education, and politics. In a culture that puts a priority on
individualism, power, and status, however, they need to
remember the gospel admonition to value the widow and
orphan, and to serve. Christians are meant to be people
whose lives of compassion and service stand in contrast
to the society that surrounds them. Unfortunately, as
Gerhard Lohfink points out, "Western...Christians are
no longer aware that the church as a whole should be an
alternative type of society."[124]

When the contrast is visible, people notice. Every
Christian need not emulate the Amish who, for the
most part, reject modern society. In October 2006, after
ten Amish schoolchildren were shot and five killed, the
response of their community stunned the world. "Within
six or seven hours of the shooting, they had gone to the
home of the gunman's widow, and his parents and in-laws
to express their sympathies for him and his death and for
the family as fellow victims."[125] The Amish could not do
otherwise. Forgiveness is central to their way of life. As
Alice Culp, a reporter for the South Bend *Tribune* points

---

122. Walter Brueggemann, *The Prophetic Imagination*, 2nd ed. (Minneapolis, MN: Fortress Press, 2001), 3.

123. Cahill, 6.

124. Lohfink, *Jesus and Community,* 125.

125. Alice Culp, "Predisposed to Forgive," *South Bend Tribune* (March 27, 2008): D1 .

out, "There is not a lot of wiggle room to explain away an otherwise hard saying of Jesus in this regard."[126]

To be a contrast society, the gospel doesn't require Christians to separate themselves from the secular world, wear different clothes, and forego technology as the Amish choose to do. It does, however, demand a different style of life, a new form of life, striving to perceive what God wants society to be and beginning to live it in the here and now. Christians can make God's peace visible through the quality of their lives. Wherever they are, they can live by kingdom principles of love, peace, justice, and forgiveness. People will notice. The quality of relationships among Christians should astonish the world, who will say, "See how they love one another"—and everyone else. Those relationships are fundamental. Those "in Christ" live within the realm of Christ's Spirit, where sin and death no longer rule. Lohfink points out, "'Being in Christ' does not mean a purely individual relationship between Christ and the believer. It means belonging to the realm within which Christ rules, and that realm is his body, the community."[127]

For this reason many people, including myself, while remaining faithful to our churches, dioceses, congregations, or denominations, have joined one of the many new intentional Christian communities. Some have even begun such communities. Living this way intensifies our call to live as the body of Christ, our vocation, our call from God to hold our lives more in common. This is the way we see the Church: God intends that men and women, who have received the gospel of Jesus Christ and who have been given the free gifts of faith and saving grace, form the Body

126. Ibid..
127. Lohfink, *Does God*, 259 and 260.

of Christ. We are responding to his action—his call, his initiation to bring us together. Throughout the history of the Church, those who believe in Jesus are not called into relationship with him as isolated individuals; in Him and through Him, He intends that they relate to one another as brothers and sisters. In Jesus we belong to one another, so that those who have accepted Jesus Christ find their proper and full place in him only when properly related to one another in his body, into *koinonia*, fellowship, community, a network of strong personal relationships.

Their common life spurs these Christians to be co-creators with Christ in the Father's plan to bring about a new heaven and a new earth. Such "communities" strive to embody kingdom principles in their daily life. God's righteousness and justice manifest themselves in tolerance, loving service, and sharing goods and possessions. These visible "instances" of the kingdom can lead to peace because they are schools for learning conflict resolution, and because they provide an alternative to the negative values often found in society at large.

Although in itself the concept of a contrast society is not biblical, the Christian vision of such a society emerges from the Old Testament. In a contrast society, "Israel" signifies not a geographical location, but the fullness of the people of God, distinct from all other peoples of the earth. Yet "Israel" is not meant to be like Qumran, an elitist society that looked down on all others, removed from daily life and society.[128] The world can be changed, Lohfink, believes, only when the people of God itself changes. "It is not possible to preach social repentance to others unless one lives in a community which takes seriously the new

---

128. Lohfink, *Jesus and Community*, 134,135.

society of the reign of God."[129] He himself lives in such a community, the *Integrierte Gemeinde* in Munich, where he has found "a common life and exchange such as I had never experienced before."[130]

Cahill goes so far as to suggest relating kingdom discipleship to social responsibility through the "formation of communities that are analogous to the biblical communities in terms of their challenge to standard patterns of social living."[131] This was the approach of Dorothy Day in founding the Catholic Worker houses. She believed that ultimately, pacifism is not supported by intellectual arguments alone but by a radical way of life lived with integrity. "The only answer in this life to the loneliness we are all bound to feel is community. The living together, working together, sharing together, loving God and loving our brother, and living close to him in community so we can show our love for Him."[132] Without such community, Dietrich Bonhoeffer said, the world has no way of knowing that all of God's creation is meant to live in peace.[133]

Such communities provide a genuine and compelling contrast to the wider community. They are a living "instance" of the body of Christ on the earth, a model of what life in the kingdom can be like. Walter Wink says that in such communities "the reign of God is not 'built' but sampled. We have a foretaste, an appetizer...a down

129. Ibid., 138.

130. Lohfink, *Does God...*, 134.

131. Cahill, 14.

132. Dorothy Day, *The Long Loneliness* (New York: Harper and Row, 1952, 1981), 243.

133. Dietrich Bonhoeffer, "No Rusty Swords," http://www.ecunet.de/gerecht/one.book/index.html?entry=page.book.1.2.3.

payment."[134] In particular, charismatic covenant communities see the "reign of God" breaking in as the essential
signs and wonders of the New Testament communities
are experienced again. Miracles, healing, and deliverance
occur and attract. Lohfink prophesies, "When Christian
communities are again transformed into true communities, wonders will begin anew."[135]

Have Christians, individually or as communities, acted
upon their convictions as one united body? Rarely. The
abortion debate may have begun to nudge them into
solidarity. More than any other "issue," the right to life
of the preborn has energized and united many Christian
people to see that **decisions, legislation, or actions that
the state permits as legal may be immoral and demand
opposition**. Furthermore, years of pro-life activism have
demonstrated that opposition cannot remain private. It
is not enough to say, "I'm opposed, but others should be
able do what they want." Hiding behind moral relativism
is not putting on the mind of Christ. Christianity is not
a private religion. It is intimately bound up with a social
agenda, because the kingdom that Christ is establishing
among and through people is being built in the concrete,
real world where they live.

Christians are not waiting to get out of this messy
world, but are working in the here and now to change the
mess, to usher in the kingdom, the new heaven and new
earth that is being established and ordered on justice, righteousness, love, and peace. Love of enemies is at the center
of that kingdom and at the heart of the gospel. Indeed,

---

134. Walter Wink, *Engaging the Powers* (Minneapolis, MN: Fortress Press,
    1992), 70.
135. Lohfink, *Jesus and Community*, 87.

Christians should consider no one an enemy. Novelist and humorist Anne Lamott points out the inherent contradiction in labeling someone as an enemy: "You can safely assume that you've created God in your own image when it turns out that God hates all the same people you do."[136]

Confessing that the way of Christ implies an anti-war position is difficult. Nevertheless, as Jim Wallis explains, "Faithfully confessing Christ is the church's task, and never more so than when its confession is co-opted by militarism and nationalism."[137] Peace does not mean avoiding difficulty. In an interview with Dolores Del Rio, Johnny Carson asked the Mexican actress, then over seventy years old, the secret of her flawless skin. She said she had decided years ago "never to laugh or smile too broadly, nor to frown or cry without restraint." Sadly, Del Rio had achieved a kind of peace by avoidance, rather than positive action. By not showing laughter or sorrow, she had consigned herself to an emotional void rather than living life to the fullest.

Some take the Del Rio approach to the difficulties and challenges of living out the gospel. Do nothing excessive, nothing radical, just lie low and hope to make it through unscathed. True Christianity calls for the opposite. Christians are called to be radicals, revolutionaries, to stick their heads out, to be the light of the world. Because everything matters, they become involved in law, politics, education, culture, in the very governing of society. Christians have a "stake" in the world; they cannot "opt out." Cahill has noted that the community to which Christians belong

---

136. Anne Lamott, *Bird by Bird*, quoted Joshua Casteel,70.
137. Jim Wallis, "Contesting a theology of war confessing Christ in a world of violence," *Catholic New Times* (5 December 2004), http://findarticles.com/p/articles/mi_m0MKY/is_19_28/ai_n8698007/?tag=content;col1.

is not merely religious, but social, cultural and political. This pluralism in Christian identity has always posed the problem of where to place allegiance or how to "reconcile competing allegiances and responsibilities."[138]

Christians differ in how to do this. A 2009 *New York Times* headline reads "Pastor Urges His Flock to Bring Guns to Church." Ken Pagano, pastor of the New Bethel Church in Louisville, Kentucky, invited his congregation to bring their firearms into the sanctuary to "celebrate our rights as Americans!" He claimed to see no contradiction with Christianity in what he was doing, calling his critics' arguments "baloney." At the other end of the spectrum, John Phillips, pastor of the Central Church of Christ in Little Rock, Arkansas, responded "I don't understand how any minister who is familiar with the teachings of the Bible can do this. Jesus didn't say, 'Go ahead, make my day.'"[139]

Reflecting on the Beatitudes, in a sermon to Benedict XVI's papal household, Fr. Raniero Cantalamessa stated that "the gospel leaves no room for doubt about non-violence as the proper Christian attitude."[140] Even if over the centuries some Christians have not always lived up to these ideals, Fr. Cantalamessa states that the gospel clearly witnesses to non-violence.

Choosing to "turn the other cheek" conjures up thoughts of martyrdom. Non-violence can be frightening, "because the making of peace is at least as costly as the making of war—at least as exigent, at least as disruptive,

---

138. Cahill, ix.
139. Katharine Q Seelye, "Pastor Urges His Flock to Bring Guns to Church," *New York Times* (June 26, 2009): A1.
140. Quoted by John L. Allen Jr., *National Catholic Reporter* Conversation Café (16 March 2007), http://ncrcafe.org/node/978.

at least as liable to bring disgrace and prison and death in its wake."[141] Whom do Christians serve? The principles of Christ's Kingdom are clear. "Servanthood replaces dominion; forgiveness absorbs hostility."[142] Such principles cannot be reconciled with a secular culture of war. Will Christians be marked with the sign of this cross? Even those who choose gospel non-violence as their response to personal enemies hesitate to apply this "Jesus approach" in national affairs. Personal and public morality may well have different bases, but individuals must exercise moral responsibility for themselves. The Christian humanist Erasmus posed this question: "How can you say 'Our Father,' while you are thrusting the sharp steel into the body of your brother?"[143] Church and State are separate, but Christian citizens' consciences should at least be stirred. They should be willing to ponder the disparity between personal and public approaches to violence and warfare. Miroslav Volf suggests, "Having been embraced by God we must make space for others in ourselves and invite them in—even our enemies. This is what we enact as we celebrate the Eucharist. In receiving Christ's broken body and spilled blood, we, in a sense, receive all those whom Christ received by suffering"[144]

Stanley Hauerwas, a United Methodist theologian, explains the connection between the Eucharist and Christians' public lives. "If Christians leave the Eucharistic

141. Daniel Berrigan, http://www.brainyquote.com/quotes/quotes/d/danielberr304318.html.

142. John Howard Yoder, *The Politics of Jesus* (Grand Rapids, MI:Eerdmans, 1972), 134.

143. Quoted in Geoffrey Nuttall, *Christian Pacifism in History* (Berkeley, CA: Basil Blackwell & Mott, 1958), 58.

144. Volf, 129.

table ready to kill one another, we not only eat and drink judgment on ourselves, but we rob the world of the witness necessary for the world to know there is an alternative to the sacrifices of war."[145] If, as they are sent out from the table of the Lord, Christians recognize their true identity and their mission, if they are fully aware of who they are in Christ and their power in the Spirit, if they are more united, they can make a difference.

145. Stanley Hauerwas, "Sacrificing the Sacrifices of War," *Journal of Religion, Conflict and Peace* (Fall, 2007}: 1.

VI

War Within the Church

John Howard Yoder has said "The need is for what [Christians] do in the world to be different because they are Christian." The starting place for such a distinctive lifestyle must surely be at home within the church's own life.[146]

I find war is repugnant, so it troubled me when, during a lecture at the University of Notre Dame a few years ago, Helen Hull Hitchcock (founder of Women for Faith and Family) declared that there is a "war" within the Church. Certainly, she was using the word analogically, but I was still upset because the older I get and the more battle scars I accumulate, the more certain I am that we Christians must find new ways to disagree with one another. If Christians hope for a less bellicose world, they must begin "at home." The increasingly hostile polarization among Christians on the "right" and on the "left," particularly within my own Catholic Church produces no useful result. Even more painful is the confusion and scandal this conflict causes in the world for which Jesus Christ died, the very world he entrusted to those who bear his name.

This disheartening, acrimonious "war" destroys through its dearth of dialogue and charity. And I, too,

---

146. Alastair McKay, "Building a Contrast Society," *Bridgebuilders Annual Report*, http://www.menno.org.uk/pdf/BBannualreport2005-2006.pdf.

am guilty. Although I call myself a quasi-pacifist, reading Ecclesiasticus 28:18 makes me cringe: "Many have fallen by the edge of the sword, but not as many as have fallen because of the tongue." Perhaps my own repentant attempt to be more open has made me more sensitive to the lapses I notice in myself and in others.

At the Catholic conference where Hitchcock spoke, most of the speakers represented a "conservative" Perspective. I share their concern about the state of the Church today, but the general tone saddened me. Certain names (usually liberal nuns known for promoting a feminist agenda) drew hoots and derisive remarks. Speakers protested that they had been labeled "mean-spirited" because they criticized those who they considered to be "undermining traditional values." Yet some (not all) indeed were mean-spirited.

Nor are the "liberals" who label these conservatives as mean-spirited any less vicious. Derisive comments about those who hold orthodox or traditional views are common. Orthodoxy is deemed "fundamentalism," and tradition "the oppressor." Those who hold orthodox or traditional viewpoints face great contempt. The "debate" between the two "camps" consists not in dialogue, but in name-calling. Yet St. Ignatius, that former soldier, reminds Christians that their choice is between the camp of Jesus and the camp of the enemy. Why should those within the same camp of Jesus become enemies? What is needed, Gerhard Lohfink suggests, is "not a church without conflicts, but a church in which conflicts are settled in ways different from the rest of society."[147]

---

147. McKay

Oblate Fr. Ron Rolheiser has spoken in much the same vein. Speaking to the Paulist Fathers on the 150th anniversary of their order, he urged them to position themselves "beyond liberal, beyond conservative" with respect to the ideological infighting in Catholicism that followed the Second Vatican Council. Catholics, he said, need balance. A balanced Catholic, Rolheiser argued, should be ready both "to lead a peace march and to lead the rosary." Too often, he suggested, they feel that they must choose either social activism or a deep spiritual life, when in fact the two belong together.[148]

Catholics are not alone in being so divided. The Christian world everywhere is splintered with rivalries. Sadly, the scandal of division and lack of ecumenical cooperation stalls evangelization. Christians tend to label each other according to perceived ideological differences, but labels block unity. Truth resists all labels. Individuals can and do differ with one another in substantial ways, and every person's "opinion" deserves respect. Moreover, individuals can differ within themselves. The same person may hold "conservative" and "liberal" opinions. If, for example someone opposes both abortion and sending troops to the Middle East, is she conservative or liberal? In terms of politics, the two stances are irreconcilable; in terms of love, however, they are coherent. Love finds a way for people who differ to listen to one another. Those at odds with one another over opposing issues can seem like "enemies." According to Matthew's Gospel, however, those who would remain a friend of God forgive their enemies, love and pray for them.

---

148. John L. Allen, Jr., "All Things Catholic," *National Catholic Reporter* (June 2008), http://ncrcafe.org/node/1941

How can Christians make their love practical? Recently, pastors and Christian leaders from across the political and theological spectrum composed a *Covenant for Civility*, which many organizations and individuals have signed. The *Covenant* notes that the church in the United States is capable of offering a message of hope and reconciliation to a nation deeply divided by political and cultural differences; nevertheless, it often reflects the political divisions of American culture rather than the unity of the body of Christ. It calls for a moral debate in which parties that disagree do so respectfully, without impugning each other's motives or character, and without questioning one another's faith.

My experience of almost forty years in an ecumenical, covenant community has shown me that Christians can stand on opposite sides of a theological divide and argue, yet remain loyal to one another and to the truth. Divisions can be handled in love—with right speech—because at root, holiness is about charity. Saints may not always be clear in their thinking and may not have a "corner on the truth." In fact, they can even be wrong. St. Robert Bellarmine, for example, was mistaken about Galileo, but he gave the poor everything he had—his money, food and possessions—and was known for his humility.[149] Saints are not canonized because of their intelligence or skill in argument, but because of their holiness. Realizing that should give all of us hope.

For years, the young upstart Augustine and the aging curmudgeon Jerome sparred over Jerome's translation of the scriptures. But because Augustine's arguments had

---

149. James Brodrick,S.J, *Robert Bellarmine* (Westminster: Newman Press, 1961), 235,385,398.

rescued the Church from the perils of Pelagianism, Jerome sent him a glowing letter of praise.[150]   Both are saints. Although they often disagreed, they were united in their overwhelming love for the Lord and their loyalty to his Church, which they had pledged themselves to defend.

The non-violent solution to the war within the Church and among the churches wells up from a love of God greater than that for ourselves or our cause. It will be manifest in a willingness to follow the Holy Spirit who leads the Church to truth. Those who can be open to the Spirit can truly listen to those with whom they disagree, can truly hear opinions that differ from their own. Putting on the mind of Christ takes humility. Transformation in Christ will often mean "changing our minds."   Human beings resist having to say "I was wrong," yet both repentance and intellectual honesty sometimes demand it.

When I was a freshman at Duquesne University I was quite conservative politically, an ardent fan of Ayn Rand's novels and her ideology of individualism.   Then, one day, I found myself sitting on a classroom floor listening to Dorothy Day. I left that room a different person. No lecture reshaped me so thoroughly as that one in the fall of 1960.

"Who is Dorothy Day, anyway?" I asked my friend as we planted ourselves in the corner of the large, crowded classroom. What she told me—her writing for various Socialist newspapers, founding "houses of hospitality" for vagrants, advocacy for pacifism—didn't impress me. The room was crammed and I was already uncomfort-

---

150. Pope Benedict XV, *Spiritus paraclitus* (On St. Jerome), http://www.papalencyclicals.net/Ben15/b15spiri.htm.

able and beginning to wish I hadn't come. Day began to speak, her voice halting, measured, barely audible. When a space cleared among the tangle of people in front of me, I caught a glimpse of her. Perched unceremoniously on a tall wooden stool, long legs crossed, sat "the radical fanatic," her grey hair pulled up in braids that wound across the top of her head. She didn't look like a fanatic, but if "radical" means exposing the root of a difficulty and advocating extreme measures, she certainly was radical. She struck a deep nerve. As I listened, I felt a pain within that throbbed like a toothache.

On one level, Day had made me confront a previously hidden ideology and world-view. I was politically naïve. I knew nothing about poverty and pacifism, but I met them in this elderly woman's words and in her eyes. What she said filled me with fear and confusion and even anger. It hurt. In her I saw what it meant to be truly "poor in spirit," filled to overflowing with a peace for which I hungered. She exuded peace, even in the face of hostile remarks that welled up in that crowded classroom after her talk. It was clear she'd encountered them before. Peace sat with her. She called him Jesus. His coming to earth announced "peace on earth," and he was sent so that the poor might have good news preached to them. His mission became hers. No pain, persecution, impoverishment or imprisonment prevented her from doing what she had come to perceive not only as God's will, but as God's way.

Afterward, I bantered with the professor who had arranged for her to come. "Is she crazy or what?" He looked at me with unusual seriousness and said, "She is either crazy or quite possibly a saint." A saint. Perhaps that's what it is, I thought, that lofty idealism and a quiet, passionate, burning zeal for following the Lord whatever the cost.

Perhaps even this saint had some wrong ideas, but I doubt it. I have come to share many of the ideals that Dorothy Day preached and lived. The poverty part is tough. My zeal often stalls, but I'm working on it. Would that there were fewer verbal tennis matches about peace and more witnesses to living it. Radicals. Saints, perhaps. It could change the world. Truth, spoken by saints, moves the soul.

Dorothy Day moved me from "conservative" individualism to "liberal" evangelical poverty and pacifism. At another point in my life, however, the "truth" moved me from a "liberal" ideological position to a more "conservative" one. In the late 1960's I was invited to serve on the board of a local Planned Parenthood chapter. At the time I was teaching in a Catholic high school, had developed a "free university" sex education class, was a representative of LaLeche League, and was teaching Lamaze natural childbirth classes. In those pre-*Roe v Wade* days, my interest in teaching, sexuality, childbirth, and motherhood seemed a natural fit with Planned Parenthood's agenda. At a certain point, however, the president of Planned Parenthood, Alan F. Guttmacher, began to promote the preparation for what he said was a "soon coming" bill that would legalize abortion. I resigned. I could not possibly compromise on that issue.

But I had been willing to compromise on other issues related to sexuality. Even though I was a Catholic, I felt no conflict in joining the Planned Parenthood board because in the days before *Humane vitae*, many of us in and around Catholic universities had *assumed* that the Church was about to change its teaching on birth control. Imagine our shock when the majority recommendation of the papal commission established to study the subject recommended the change, but Pope Paul VI rejected it. With great difficulty, but with the relentless urging of the Holy Spirit, I yielded (eventually and uneasily) to the teaching of *Humane vitae*. Changing one's mind is rarely easy.

Are those who think differently than we do our enemies? If so, are they God's enemies too? Perhaps. But Ignatius of Loyola suggests that those with whom we differ may well be God's instruments. Pruning. Purifying. Testing. The enemy is not "others," but God's one, ancient, personal enemy whose kingdom is marked by darkness, lies and division. To defeat that real enemy, all within the church of Jesus must talk and laugh and work together so love can triumph. Who gloats over our divisions and goads us to continue in them? Not the merciful God and Father of our Lord Jesus Christ. Unity within the Catholic Church and unity among all the churches and people of God is, therefore, the prerequisite for facing the world's challenges. For Christians to be a contrast society, people must see how they love one another.

One of those challenges is nuclear warfare. Prophetic voices, Catholic and Protestant, have been speaking out to nudge the people of God toward this "other," sometimes uncomfortable, non-violent point of view. Dorothy Day, Thomas Merton, Gordon Zahn, Philip and Daniel Berrigan, John Howard Yoder, Stanley Hauerwas, Michael Baxter, Richard Hayes, Fr. Gerhard Lohfink, Lisa S. Cahill: these are some of the prophets of non-violence. Pope Francis is another. Perhaps the sad and contentious reaction of some in the Church to his papacy will serve as a strong example of the divide we face. Headlines like this are not unusual: "Conservative Roman Catholic theologians accuse pope of spreading heresy"[151]

Some Christians may not agree with the methods or with the conclusions of these "prophets," but their voices have a place in any serious discussion of the church's relationship to society. Perhaps such a discussion on peace can be conducted with peace.

151. http://www.chicagotribune.com/news/nationworld/ct-conservative-theologians-pope-heresy-20170923-story.html.

VII

Blessed are the Peacemakers

In times of war, you often hear leaders—Christian, Jewish, and Muslim—saying, "God is on our side." But that isn't true. In war, God is on the side of refugees, widows, and orphans.[152]

St. Paul wrote to the Christian community of Rome, "If it is possible, so far as it depends on you, live peaceably with all" (Rom 12:18). Even in apostolic times, what is "possible" in the Christian response seems to have been limited. Why? Do Christians consider the reality of being members of the body of Christ in this world secondary to being citizens of the state ? Have they accepted an unnecessary dichotomy? Have they lost their sense of the cost of discipleship? Have they become walking contradictions, preaching the gospel of the Prince of Peace and Lord of Life while condoning war?

Some, like Richard Hays, emphasize the limits that the church has placed upon itself in seeking the "possible." He claims that Christianity is "deeply compromised and committed to nationalism, violence...liberation theologies that justify violence against oppressors, and...establishment Christianity that continues to play chaplain to the military industrial complex, citing just war theory and

---

152. Greg Mortenson and David Oliver Relin, *Three Cups of Tea* (New York: Penguin Books, 2006), 239.

advocating the defense of a particular nation as though that were somehow a Christian value."[153] Hays claims that the whole of the Church is committed to violence, but the many statements from bishops and recent popes suggest otherwise.

Others, like N.T. Wright, see the church as answering the call of the gospel to implement the victory of God by his Spirit and through his people. Paradoxically, this victory will be accomplished not through power, but through suffering and martyrdom. "The suffering love of God, lived out again by the Spirit in the lives of God's people, is the God-given answer to the evils of the world."[154]

The corporal works of mercy—feeding the hungry, housing the homeless, clothing the naked, healing the sick, visiting prisoners—constitute peacemaking. So too is the development of social systems that make the world a better place to live, because peacemaking requires Christians to take action in the political sphere. Lisa Cahill notes, "The church is to be the advocate in the political arena for the idea of *shalom* yielded by the scriptures."[155] But they must do even more. Fr. Raniero Cantalamessa also emphasizes that the seventh beatitude is not about Christian identity, but about Christian action. Peacemaking, he says, is having "no fear of compromising...personal peace by intervening in conflicts to help those who are divided to find peace."[156] Such work is demanding.

What, for example, does the Eucharist mean in Rwanda, where members of the same parish were

153. Hays, 343.
154. N.T. Wright, "God, 9/11, the Tsunami and the New Problem of Evil."
155. Cahill, 6.
156. Rainero Cantalamessa, OFM.,Cap.,Advent Sermon, December, 2006.

both perpetrators and victims of genocide-and
in some cases, both? How does a pastor in rural
Colombia talk to his parishioners about the sac-
rament of reconciliation when the pews are filled
with paramilitaries who have committed war
crimes, as well as parishioners who were victim-
ized by them?[157]

This often dangerous work requires courage and the
power of the Spirit. In addition, it requires ecumenical
cooperation. For example, in northern Uganda, where the
Lord's Resistance Army has terrorized the local population, "Catholic Archbishop John Baptist Odama of Gulu
and his Muslim, Orthodox and Anglican counterparts
have even gone into the bush, at great risk to themselves,
to meet with the ruthless leaders of the LRA."[158]

Many Christians today advocate actively for peace.
Members of the Sant'Egidio Community, a Catholic
lay movement whose charism is serving the poor, work
as peacemakers in many places, most notably in Darfur,
Sudan. They have brought Sudanese combatants to Rome,
in order to facilitate political negotiations. Their interven-
tions work because they act as an external party without
personal interests or hidden agendas. In Peru, the Catholic
bishops have agreed to mediate between indigenous
Amazonian communities and the police. Since 1984,
Chicago-based Christian Peacemaker Teams, including
Mennonites, members of the Church of the Brethren, and

---

157. Powers,15.
158. Powers,16.

Quakers, have traveled to Columbia, Iraq, various African countries, and to Israel and the West Bank to offer their lived witness of the possibility of peace.

Some just war advocates and pacifists build peace by establishing just conditions wherever they are. According to the *Catechism of the Catholic Church*, injustice, economic or social inequality, and personal or national pride threaten peace and cause wars. Whatever can be done, therefore, "to overcome these disorders contributes to building up peace and avoiding war..."[159] Citing the *Pastoral Constitution of the Church in the Modern World*, the *Catechism* notes in addition that "insofar as they can vanquish sin by coming together in charity, violence itself will be vanquished."[160] Such convictions come at a high cost. Archbishop Oscar Romero of El Salvador was assassinated for his insistence that "if we really want an effective end to violence, we must remove the violence that lies at the root...: structural violence, social injustice, exclusion of citizens from the management of the country, repression."[161]

Josh Casteel, who been face to face with those who would use terror as a weapon, held the same opinion. "Humanitarian assistance is our best weapon against terrorism—to give the terrorists no social or economic foothold into the weaknesses of the poor."[162] Fear must not prevent working for justice. Together, non-violent resistance to injustice and non-violent humanitarian

---

159. *Catechism of the Catholic Church* #2317.

160. Ibid., #2317.

161. Bishop Oscar Romero, *The Violence of Love*, ed. James Brochman,(San Francisco: Harper and Row, 1988),43.

162. Casteel, 22,23.

intervention can lead toward the abolition of war.[163] Greg
Mortenson promotes peace by building schools throughout Afghanistan and Pakistan. He notes, "If we truly want
a legacy of peace for our children, we need to understand
that this is a war that will ultimately be won with books,
not with bombs."[164] Fr. Elias Chacour is attempting to
wage just such a war. He runs a school near Nazareth where
Palestinian Christians, Jews, and Muslims are educated
together. His book *Blood Brother* conveys his wisdom and
passion for peacemaking.[165]

Gerard Powers, of the Institute for Peace Studies at the
University of Notre Dame, describes the Catholic Church's
efforts in the Philippines:

> [They are in the] forefront of ... peacebuilding
> efforts—trying to overcome the deep histori-
> cal divide between Christians, Muslims and the
> indigenous peoples, called the Lumad, through
> inter-religious dialogue, efforts to address the eco-
> nomic, social and political marginalization of the
> Muslims and Lumads, and by a range of efforts
> designed to cultivate a culture of peace in a region
> that has known little but war for generations.[166]

He describes the situation in the Philippines as
"emblematic of a subtle but important development in

---

163. *A Call for Conversation: Seeking Justice and Peace through Non-violence
     and Abolition of War*, a study and reflection paper presented to the
     Presbytery of Greater Atlanta, http://www.presbyteryofgreateratl.org/
     ministry_teams/outreach/peacemaking/alternativepaper-Maydraft.htm.

164. Mortenson, 301.

165. Elias Chacour, with David Hazard, *Blood Brothers* (Grand Rapids, MI:
     Chosen Books, 2003).

166. Gerard Powers, "Catholic Peacebuilding," 13

Catholic thinking and pastoral practice related to war and peace—a new focus on peacebuilding."[167] By peacebuilding he means the "broad range of non-violent activities involved in preventing conflicts from erupting into violence, managing and trying to resolve violent conflicts once they erupt, and promoting reconstruction and reconciliation after violent conflicts have ended."[168] By itself, peacebuilding cannot resolve the debate between just war tradition and pacifism. It can provide, however, a basis for common ground among the church's varied approaches to war and peace. "Peacebuilding is not a replacement for the just war tradition, but is a necessary complement to it."[169]

Some propose a world without nuclear weapons. In "Thinking the Unthinkable," Carla Robbins notes that George Shultz, Henry Kissinger, William Perry, and Sam Nunn, men not given to "casual utopianism," have called on the United States to lead a global campaign to reduce the number of nuclear weapons, and eventually rid the world of them. At the 1986 Reykjavik summit, when Ronald Reagan proposed abolishing nuclear weapons, James Schlesinger and Margaret Thatcher criticized him as having a "lack of understanding of strategic exigencies."[170] In a frightening world marked by ever-expanding nuclear appetites, however, traditional deterrence no longer works. Shultz and the others argue that the United States can rally the cooperation it needs to confront such dangers only through with a "clear commitment to the goal of a

---

167. Ibid.
168. Ibid.
169. Ibid., 14.
170. Carla Anne Robbins. *New York Times*. June 30, 2008.

world without nuclear weapons."[171] **Christians who may otherwise disagree about the justifiability of war can work together for peace through this "third way."** Through such a "third way," proponents of just war as well as those who see war as unjustifiable find common ground in their desire to secure conditions that make war less likely.[172] Christians are not meant to embrace what Stanley Hauerwas calls a "withdrawal ethic," so such discussions risk being subsumed into political agendas. However, Hauerwas notes, as people of God Christians are called to

> Develop the resources to stand within the world witnessing to the peaceable kingdom, and thus rightly understanding the world. The gospel is a political gospel…a politics of the kingdom that reveals the insufficiency of all politics based on coercion and falsehood and finds the true source of power in servanthood rather than domination.[173]

Because peacemaking is inescapably political, the Methodist Bishops' Council has urged Christians to work toward "changing the policies and perhaps some of the leaders and structures of government."[174] The church itself must work as peacemaker in order to be "the advocate in the political arena for the idea of *shalom* yielded by the scriptures."[175] At the very least the church should support efforts to limit the arms race and suspend the proliferation

171. Robbins. "Thinking the Unthinkable…"

172. *A Call for Conversation.*

173. Stanley Hauerwas, *Peaceable Kingdom: A Primer in Christian Ethics* (Notre Dame, IN: University of Notre Dame Press, 1983), 102.

174. Methodist Bishops Council, *In Defense of Creation: The Nuclear Crisis and a Just Peace* (Nashville, TN: Graded Press, 1986),88.

175. Cahill, 6.

of nuclear weapons. Pope Paul VI said, "The arms race is to be condemned unreservedly. It is itself an act of aggression...for even when they are not used, by their cost alone, armaments kill the poor by causing them to starve."[176] In a letter to President Barack Obama praising the April 8, 2010, signing of the Strategic Arms Reduction Treaty, Cardinal Francis George of Chicago, President of the United States Conference of Catholic Bishops reinforced the Church's stand against nuclear arms. "The horribly destructive capacity of nuclear arms makes them disproportionate and indiscriminate weapons that endanger human life and dignity like no other armaments. Their use as a weapon of war is rejected in Church teaching based on just war norms."[177]

Christians work for peace, however, not because of their political stance, but because of their moral conviction. The United States Conference of Catholic Bishops asserts that

> Peacemaking is not an optional commitment. It is a requirement of our faith. We are called to be peacemakers, not by some movement of the moment, but by our Lord Jesus. The content and context of our peacemaking is set not by some political agenda or ideological program, but by the teaching of his Church.[178]

---

176. Pope Paul VI. 1975 Vatican "Statement on Disarmament," http://www.vatican.va/holy_father/paul_vi/messages/peace/documents/hf_p-vi_mes_19751018_ix-world-day-for-peace_en.html.

177. http://www.usccb.org/sdwp/international/2010-04-08-let-card-george-pres-obama.pdf.

178. NCCB, *Pastoral Letter on War and Peace.*

Such a task seems insurmountable in the face of global threats to peace—genocide, terrorism, and the confrontation between a Western worldview and that of Islamic extremists. Bruce Bawer's *While Europe Slept*,[179] for example, which documents the breadth and depth of radical Islam in Europe, exemplifies the ideological divide and the potential for violence in this encounter. Joshua Casteel warns, however, "If we approach the war on terrorism with the fervor of a Christian Jihad against Islam, our battle is already lost, for we have become what we opposed and we are now the fundamentalists."[180]

The evil in the world has many faces. "To enjoy the taste of our eventual deliverance from evil" each person needs to learn how to "loose the bonds of evil in the present."[181] Exercising that lesson requires shrewdness and discernment. Bonhoeffer has pointed out how easy it is to confuse peace with safety. "For Peace must be dared. It is the great venture. It can never be safe. Peace is the opposite of security. To demand guarantees is to mistrust and this mistrust in turn brings forth war."[182] Launching retaliatory war in the name of security cannot be the Lord's way. Mimicking terrorists in their use of violence will only generate more hate. "Means are always ends in process, as Gandhi, King and Jesus tried to teach us. So killing ter-

---

179. Bruce Bawer, *While Europe Slept: How Radical Islam is Destroying the West from Within* (New York: Broadway Books,2006).

180. Casteel,71.

181. N.T. Wright, *Evil and the Justice of God* (Downers Grove, IL: IVP Books, 2006),147.

182. Dietrich Bonhoffer, *The Essential Writings of Dietrich Bonhoeffer*, Geffrey B. Kelley and F. Burton Nelson, eds. (New York: Harper Collins, 1995), 228.

rorists in terrible ways…will not kill terrorism, but feed it. Security secured in this way is the opposite of peace."[183]

Christians face the difficult, puzzling, yet urgent task of discovering "the practical ways in today's and tomorrow's world of seeking justice without violence, of making and maintaining peace without tyranny."[184] I feel hope because in my own lifetime I have seen the world change through the non-violent action of Christians and non-Christians alike: Gandhi in India, Desmond Tutu in South Africa and Martin Luther King in Selma, Alabama. Their inevitable suffering brought certain victory. No one can excuse himself or herself from the struggle by saying, "But I am not Ghandi or Tutu or King." The movie *Pray the Devil Back to Hell* documents ordinary Liberian women who brought peace to their country. Thousands, Christian and Muslim, united in their prayer for peace, protested silently outside of the presidential palace in Monrovia. As one review notes, "armed only with white T-shirts and the courage of their convictions," they demanded a resolution to the country's bloody civil war.[185] Their actions were critical in restarting the stalled peace talks and bringing about a settlement.

Christians should heed the example of those who have found practical ways of seeking justice without tyranny. Upon reading *Three Cups of Tea,* Deborah Mullen (wife of Admiral Mike Mullen, then Chairman of the Joint Chiefs of Staff) and Holly Petraeus (wife of General David

183. Larry Rasmussen, Reinhold Niebuhr Professor of Social Ethics at Union Theological Seminary. Unpublished statement on the World Trade Center attack, September 20, 2001.

184. N.T. Wright, "The Prince of Peace," November 13, 2005, http://www. ntwrightpage.com/sermons/Prince_Peace.htm.

185. http://www.praythedevilbacktohell.com/synopsis.php.

Petraeus, commander of American forces in Iraq and in Afghanistan) urged their husbands to meet with the book's author, Greg Mortenson, to discuss how to translate the theory of counterinsurgency into tribal realities on the ground. *Three Cups of Tea* is now on the required reading lists for senior American military commanders.[186]

The salvific suffering of Jesus himself, who responded to evil nonviolently, is the model for every Christian. Human life and activity rooted in economic, political and cultural unrighteousness comprise the "world" that hates Christ and those who follow him. Opposing this world will incur its hatred, but Jesus promised that the kingdom of heaven will belong to those persecuted for righteousness' sake (Mt 5:10). As a "sign of contradiction," Christians are called to oppose the unrighteousness of abortion, euthanasia, capital punishment, the arms race, and the culture of death. They also must concern themselves with economic disparity, racial discrimination, and resource shortages; they must work to bring righteousness, peace, order, beauty, and every other kingdom value to every "circle" in which they live—education, business, politics, culture, entertainment, art, music, media technology, and the Internet. Christ, risen and alive, is in them, and through them remains in the world and in each and all of these circles. In them and through them God loves the world. Christians make a difference by overcoming fear and by embracing the world with courage and with love.

The Christian call has no limits. In the view of historian Geoffrey Nuttall,

---

186. Buhmiller, Elizabeth, "Unlikely Tutor Giving Military Afghan Advice," *The New York Times*, July 17, 2010: p.A1.

> The State, government, power in the political
> and economic sense, must be brought within the
> compass of the redemption which is the deepest
> motive behind all our pacifism. Somehow we
> must learn to let the healing power of God work
> through us for the redemption of power as men
> and as nations, know power.[187]

Will the day will come "when prophets choose to
become diplomats, ambassadors of the quarrel of peace,
even ambassadors in chains (Eph: 20) for the sake of the
Gospel?"[188] Appeasement—a naive, politically correct
policy that does not distinguish between good and evil,
is inadequate before the harsh realities of civic life. But
Christians must never forget the Lord's injunction to love
their enemies. "It is through further development of a
theology, ethics and practice of peacebuilding, not further
debate on the just war versus pacifism, that the Catholic
community will be able to achieve its full potential in
becoming a 'peace Church.'"[189]

In a world where powers greater than human ones are
at work, "spiritual warfare" is an effective "weapon," if
wielded with the wisdom of Solomon and the power of the
Holy Spirit. Walter Wink suggests the value that stands
at the center of this struggle. The essence of the gospel
of love, he says, is non-violence. Therefore, Wink notes,
"Jesus' nonviolent followers should not be called pacifists,
but simply Christians."[190]

---

187. Nuttall,81.
188. Valliere, *Holy War*,157.
189. Powers,18.
190. Wink, 217.

Many do not share Wink's view of Christianity. Their "prevailing wisdom" can be so forceful that those with a differing viewpoint remain silent, just to "keep the peace." Certainly, the nonviolent option cannot be advanced through argument. That is why only now, in my grey haired 70's have I written this book. Though these views on non violence have been a passion within me for many years, I hesitated to put them into print, to put them "out there," for fear of losing many friends. The struggle for non-violence is difficult, and tiring. In Glencoe, Illinois during a discussion of peace issues among Catholic and Protestant charismatic leaders, Mennonite Bishop Nelson Littweiler was trying to explain his own church's anti-war position. As the evening wore on Bishop Littweiler, quite exhausted, told his colleagues that he thought it best to leave off trying to convince them. Retired General Ralph Hanes dissuaded him, saying, "Oh no, Nelson, keep going, stick to your guns." They laughed at the irony and the good bishop retired for the evening.

I, myself, have not always maintained his good sense or graciousness during difficult conversations on this subject. My frank words and passion certainly make me appear a most inconsistent advocate of nonviolence. I enjoyed watching "Lethal Weapon" and "24." I particularly enjoy the exquisitely violent game of football—especially Notre Dame's "Fighting Irish"! I am a living contradiction, so I understand the difficulty others have with the convictions I hold so dear. I am not unduly optimistic, but hope leads me to believe that one day the "greater works" (Jn 14:12) of those who continue the mission of Christ in this world will include peace and reconciliation. I want to be counted among them.

What are the works of Jesus? That daunting question can be answered by understanding his breathtaking promise: "The one who believes in me will also do the works that I do and, in fact, will do greater works than these, because I am going to the Father" (Jn 14:12). Jesus said that he would "bring good news to the poor...proclaim release to the captives and recovery of sight to the blind... let the oppressed go free" (Lk 4:18). He did all that and more—healing the deaf, the crippled, the lepers, and the possessed. He even raised the dead. How can those who believe in him possibly "do greater works than these"?

One answer to that question is that the works Christians perform are greater not in the nature of the events themselves, but in their number and scope. For example, far more people were brought to life in Christ after the Peter's sermon at Pentecost (3,000 in one day) than Jesus raised from the dead during his entire ministry. The "greater works," therefore, refer to the multitudes brought to the Lord by the ministry of the apostles, whose influence spread throughout the whole Roman world—well beyond the small area that Jesus called home.

That answer is logical, but there is a deeper, more powerful source for the "greater works" that Christians can perform—the Holy Spirit. Through the Spirit, Christ continues his ministry today in Christians, who have not even begun to tap that unlimited power. Those who collaborate with Jesus act as Christ, in Christ. What does Christ in them wish them do? "If you abide in me, and my words abide in you, ask for whatever you wish, and it will be done for you" (Jn 15:7). What is the "whatever" for which Christians wish?

There is more power in the life of the Spirit and greater
works for Christians than they can possibly imagine—
—"more," much more: more healing and deliverance and
serving and living among the poor, the displaced, and the
hopeless; the restoration of cities, the rebuilding of lives.[191]

I myself have seen many healings: sight restored to
girl blinded in an accident; a young man delivered from
alcohol and cocaine addiction; a heart condition reversed;
a ureter coiled dangerously around an artery straightened;
the disappearance of gangrene in an arm scheduled to be
amputated; the miraculous healing of a baby with a life-
threatening disorder and a man with a terminal illness. If
not greater than those of Jesus, these works—the results
of Spirit-aided prayer—are certainly greater than anything
human beings could do by themselves. There is always
"more."

Proceeding from the Holy Spirit, the works of the
disciples continue the ministry of Jesus. His work isn't
over. Christ lives in them by the power of the Spirit. Do
Christians believe that? Does it change the way they think
and act? John 14:12 says: "Very truly, I tell you, the one
who believes in me will also do the works that I do." A true
Christian wants to be such a "one." Becoming "one" means
putting on the mind and heart of Christ, letting him take
shape within, wanting to do what he wants to do. Then,
when such individuals pray, "signs will accompany those
who believe" (Mk 16:17). They will perform miracles.

---

191. See People of Praise Community, "Summer Life in Allendale," *Vine and
Branches Magazine* (August, 2007); "Our New City in Allendale," *Vine
and Branches Magazine* (March, 2006); "Missionary Stories from Indianapolis," *Vine and Branches Magazine* (November, 2007); "In Kingston:
Face to Face," *Vine and Branches Magazine* (January, 2008); "City-
Building Plans in Portland," *Vine and Branches Magazine* (May-June,
2006). All articles are available online at http://www.peopleofpraise.org.

Christians may be reluctant to exercise the full power of their faith over problematic situations, sickness, nature, even death.[192] But they can calm the waters—even, after a fashion, walk on the waters. They indeed have the power to change governments, to turn back armies, if that is what the Father wishes. However, they must desire those things. Only through the power of the Holy Spirit can they live in the world as the nonviolent Christ, ideally in community. Jesus' demands cannot be answered by individuals alone, because he came on earth to form a people, a new family. Lohfink believes that

> This [Christian] ethic can be fulfilled…only…by groups of people which consciously place themselves under the gospel of the reign of God and wish to be real communities of brothers and sisters…If we really wish to know if the Sermon on the Mount can be lived, we need to ask the groups and communities in which Christians not only live alongside one another, but have undertaken a journey together as the people of God. [193]

Christians who do not understand their complete identity have a blind spot. If they ache with compassion to do the very things the Father desires, they will see mountains move. Of course, Biblical scholars chalk up such language to Semitic hyperbole. The Hebrews, however, believed that the mountains supported the sky, like pillars that defined their universe. When Jesus talked about moving mountains, therefore, some believe he was suggesting

---

192. Chauncey Crandall, a Christian cardiologist, has recounted his story of a man being raised from the dead by prayer: http://www.cbn.com/700club/guests/bios/Chauncey-Crandall-091510.aspx.

193. Lohfink, *Jesus and Community*, 62,63.

that he and his followers could undermine the foundation of the world and change its very shape. For Christians such greater work is not only possible; it is necessary. If the desires of the heart do not become one with those of God, those hearts remain puny, hardened and divided, limiting the work of Christ. Mine often stands in the way. But when we and the mountains both begin to sense the presence of Christ within us, the trembling will begin.

Afterword

I have every confidence that we Christians can find healing for our blindness on the subject of warfare. This confidence comes from my own experience of physical healing. In the opening chapter of this book, I mentioned that I was diagnosed with a retinal or macular hole. All I could see was a large yellow dot surrounded by a black jagged edge. I had a genuine "blind spot." It became my inspiration for the title of this book. It became a metaphor to me for the blindness of Christians to the reality of war, a reality that is staring us right in the face. But only a proper understanding and acceptance of our true identity as Christians will heal that blind spot.

When first diagnosed with this macular hole, I was told I needed surgery. Afterwards, during a two to three week period of recovery, I would have to remain in a sitting position with my face down, staring at the floor for 23 hours a day, asleep or awake. We rented a special chair, like the kind used for those getting a massage, and I braced myself for the ordeal.

I have been living as a charismatic Catholic Christian for over fifty years and believe that charisms are real, including the gift of healing. Therefore, one of my preparations was to receive prayer with the laying on of hands for the healing of my eye. A week before the scheduled surgery, I went again to the retinal specialist. After a lengthy exam, he confirmed what I had already realized after the laying on of hands. He said, "This is really curious. It looks like your eye is getting better. I think we should postpone the surgery another month and see if that continues." I told him I knew I would be fine because I had been prayed with for healing. He did not comment. After a month of even <u>more</u> prayer for healing, I returned for another examination. The retinal specialist told me that my eye was at the very place he hoped that the surgery would have taken it. He cancelled the operation with these words: "It looks pretty darn healed to me." When I returned for a check up a year later, my regular ophthalmologist simply stated, "Wow, that hole has really closed over." That "healing" was over fifteen years ago. And at my most recent visit the ophthalmologist said, "That eye is even better now than your other eye!"

And so I have hope. Hope in the healing power of God. Hope that our corporate blindness in so many areas can be "healed." Hope too, perhaps, that this little book will cause just enough discomfort that some will be spurred to discuss more, to dialogue about this subject, to revisit previous assumptions, and to seek a fresh outpouring of the Holy Spirit, who comes to bring healing and comfort and to "renew the face of the earth."

Works Cited

Adler, Mortimer. "Does the End Ever Justify the Means?" (February, 2001), http://www.cooperativeindividualism.org/adler_does_end_justify_means.html.

Allen, John L. Jr. National Catholic Reporter Conversation Café (March 16, 2007), http://ncrcafe.org/node/978.

—— "All Things Catholic." *National Catholic Reporter* (June, 2008), http://ncrcafe.org/node/1941.

Augustine. *City of God.* Edited by David Knowles. Baltimore: Penguin Books,1972.

Bailey, Wilma Ann Bailey. *"You Shall Not Kill" or "You Shall Not Murder"? The Assault on a Biblical Text.* Minneapolis: Liturgical Press, 2005.

Bainton, Roland H. *Christian Attitudes Towards War and Peace.* Abingdon: Nashville, 1960.

—— *Early Christianity.* New Jersey: D.VanNostrand Co., 1960.

Baker, Daniel. "Letter to the Editor." *America Magazine.* December 22, 2008: 36.

Balch, David. "Review of Lohfink's *Jesus and Community.*" *Journal of Biblical Literature.* December 1987: 715-17

Barry, William A.,S.J. *A Friendship Like No Other: Experiencing God's Amazing Embrace.* Chicago: Loyola Press, 2008.

Bawer, Bruce. *While Europe Slept: How Radical Islam is Destroying the West from Within.* New York: Broadway Books, 2006.

Baxter, Michael J. "Just War and Pacifism: A 'Pacifist' Perspective in Seven Points." *Houston Catholic Worker* (June 1, 2004), https://cjd.org/2004/06/01/just-war-and-pacifism-a-pacifist-perspective-in-seven-points/

Beaman, Jay. *Pentecostal Pacifism.* Kansas: Center for Mennonite Brethren Studies, 1989.

"Baptism, Eucharist and Ministry," *Faith and Order Paper No 111.* Geneva: World Council of Churches, 1982.

Bernardin, Joseph, Cardinal. "Cardinal Bernardin's Call for a Consistent Ethic of Life." *Origins* (December 29, 1983): 491-94.

Berrigan, Daniel. http://www.brainyquote.com/quotes/quotes/d/danielberr304304.html.

Birch, Bruce C. "Old Testament Foundations for Peacemaking in the Nuclear Era. *The Christian Century.* (December 4, 1985): 115-19.

Boersma, Hans. *Violence, Hospitality and the Cross; Reappropriating the Atonement Tradition.* Grand Rapids: Baker Book House, 2006.

Bonhoffer, Diettrich."No Rusty Swords." http://www.ecunet.de/gerecht/one.book/index.html?entry=/page.book.1.2.3.

Brodrick, James, S.J. *Robert Bellarmine.* Westminster: Newman Press, 1961.

Brown, Raymond. *Death of the Messiah.* New York: Doubleday. 1994.

Broyde, Michael. "Pacifism in Jewish Law." http://www.myjewishlearning.com/ideas_belief/warpeace/War_Peace_TO/War_Pacifism_Broyde.htm.

Brueggemann, Walter. *The Prophetic Imagination.* Minneapolis: Fortress Press, 2001.

Bruni, Frank. "Threats and Responses. The Vatican; Pope Voices Opposition, His Strongest, To Iraq War." *New York Times* (January 14, 2003):12.

Buhmiller, Elizabeth, "Unlikely Tutor Giving Military Afghan Advice." *New York Times* (July 17, 2010): A1.

Byler, Dennis. *Making War and Making Peace.* Pennsylvania: Herald Press, 1989.

Cahill,Lisa Sowle. *Love Your Enemies: Discipleship, Pacifism and Just War Theory.* Minneapolis: Augusburg/Fortress, 1989.

Cantalamessa, Fr. Raniero, OFM.Cap. "Advent sermon to the Pontificial Household." (December, 2006), http://cantatedomino.blogspot.com/2006/12/father-cantalamessa-on-peacemakers.html.

Carlson, Reed Anthony. "What Is It Good For? Nonviolence in A Violent World: Part V." *Theophiliacs* (January 19, 2009).

Casteel, Joshua. *Letters from Abu Ghraib*. Ohio: Essay Press, 2000.

Catechism of the Catholic Church (Second Edition). Washington, D.C.: United States Catholic Conference, 1994.

Catholic Peace Fellowship. "The Moral Compass of Benedict XVI: Where Will His Commitment to Peace Lead Us?" *The Sign of Peace*. Spring, 2006.

Crandall, Chauncy. http://www.cbn.com/700club/guests/bios/Chauncey-Crandall-091510.aspx.

Culp, Alice. "Predisposed to Forgive." *South Bend Tribune* (March 27, 2008): D1.

Chacour, Elias. *Blood Brothers*. Grand Rapids: Chosen Books, 2003.

Chesterton, G.K. "The Unfinished Temple." *What's Wrong with the World*. New York: Dodd, Mead & Co., 1927.

Cole, Darrell. *When God Says War is Right. The Christian's Perspective on When and How to Fight*. Colorado: Waterbrook Press, 2002.

Collinge, William J., ed. *Faith in Public Life. The Annual Publication of the College Theological Society*. New York: Orbis Books, 2007.

Day, Dorothy. *The Long Loneliness*. New York: Harper and Row, 1981.

Derrett, J. *The Ascetic Discourse: An Explanation of the Sermon on the Mount*. Eilsbrunn, Germany: Ko'Amar, 1989.

Elliott, Neil. "Revisiting Augustine and Just War Theory." *Witness Magazine*, June 30, 2004.

Fahey, Joseph J. *War and the Christian Conscience*. New York: Orbis Books, 2005.

Flannery, Austin. O.P., ed. *The Basic Sixteen Documents of Vatican II*. New York: Costello Publishing Company, 1996.

Fuller, Graham E. "Pope Francis Takes On 'Just War' Theory" (April 14, 2016), https://consortiumnews.com/2016/04/14/pope-francis-takes-on-just-war-theory/.

Gaddis, Michael. *There is No Crime for Those Who Have Christ: Religion and Violence in the Christian Roman Empire.* Berkeley, CA: University of California Press, 2005.

George, Cardinal Francis. Letter to President Obama welcoming the signing of the START Treaty. http://www.usccb.org/sdwp/international/2010-04-08-let-card-george-pres-obama.pdf.

Girard, Rene. *Violence and the Sacred.* Translated by Patrick Gregory. Baltimore: John Hopkins University Press, 1977.

—— *The Girard Reader.* Edited by James G. Williams. New York: Crossroads, 1996.

Global Ethics and Religion Forum. http://www.gerforum.org/.

Goodwin, Doris Kearns. *Team of Rivals. The Political Genius of Abraham Lincoln.* New York: Simon and Schuster, 2006.

Hamm, Dennis. "The Bible and Public Life." *Faith in Public Life.* Edited by William J. Collinge. New York: Orbis Books, 2007, 33.

Hanson, Paul. "War and Peace in the Hebrew Bible." *Interpretation* (Fall, 1984): 347.

Hauerwas,, Stanley. "Sacrificing the Sacrifices of War." *Journal of Religion, Conflict and Peace* (Fall, 2007): 1.

——*Peaceable Kingdom: A Primer in Christian Ethics.* Notre Dame, IN: University of Notre Dame Press, 1983.

Hays, Richard B. *The Moral Vision of the New Testament.* San Francisco: Harper Collins, 1996.

Heering, Gerrit Jan. *The Fall of Christianity : A Study of Christianity, the State, and War.* New York: Garland Publishers, 1972.

Helgeland, John. "Christians and the Roman Army AD 173-337." *Church History* (June 1974): 149-63.

Hellwig, Monika. *The Eucharist and the Hunger of the World.* Maryland: Sheed and Ward, 1992.

Hobbs, TR. *A Time for War.* Wilmington, DE: Glazier, 1989.

Holt, Andrew. "Christian Pacifism: Early Christian Views of War" *Crusades-Encyclopedia* (Fall 2006), http://www.crusades-encyclopedia.com/christianpacifism.html.

Jeremias, Joachim. *The Sermon on the Mount.* London: The Athlone Press, 1961.

Kling, David William. *The Bible in History: How the Texts Have Shaped the Times*. London: Oxford University Press, 2004.

Lewy, Guenter. *The Catholic Church and Nazi Germany*. Cambridge, MA: DeCapo Press, 2000.

Lohfink, Gerhard. *Jesus and Community*. Philadelphia: Fortress Press, 1982.

—— *Does God Need the Church?* Minnesota: Liturgical Press, 1999.

Manchala, Deenabandhu, ed. *Nurturing Peace: Theological Reflections on Overcoming Violence*. Geneva: World Council of Churches Publications, 2005.

Martin, George. *Bringing the Gospel of Matthew to Life*. Maryland: The Word Among Us Press, 2008.

Maxwell, Ronald F. writer/director. "Gods and Generals." Warner Brothers, 2003.

McDonnell, Killian, OSB and George Montague, SM. *Christian Initiation and Baptism in the Holy Spirit: Evidence from the First Eight Centuries*. Collegeville, MN: Liturgical Press, 1991.

McHugh, O.P. John A. and Charles J. Callan, O.P. *Moral Theology on War*. New York: Joseph F. Wagner, Inc., 1958.

McKay, Alistair. "Building a Contrast Society." *Bridgebuilders Annual Report*, 2005-2006. http://www.menno.org.uk/pdf/ BBannualreport2005-2006.pdf.

McSorley, Richard. S.J. *It's a Sin to Build a Nuclear Weapon*. Eugene, OR: Wipf and Stock,1991.

Mennonite Statement and Study on Violence. "And No One Shall Make Them Afraid." *General Conference Mennonite Church*, 1997. http://www.gameo.org/encyclopedia/contents/A535. html.

Methodist Bishops Council. "In Defense of Creation: The Nuclear Crisis and a Just Peace." Nashville, TN: Graded Press, 1986.

Mills, C. Wright. *The Causes of World War Three*. New York: Ballantine Books, 1960.

Montague, George T. *Companion God: A Cross Cultural Commentary on the Gospel of Matthew*. New York: Paulist Press, 1989.

—— "Paul, Lone Ranger or Community Builder?" *Pentecost Today* (July/August/September 2008): 5.

Mortenson, Greg, and David Oliver Relin. *Three Cups of Tea*. New York: Penguin Books, 2006.

Muraskin, Bennett. "Secular Jews and Pacifism." http://www.csjo. org/pages/essays/essaypacifismbennett.htm.

National Conference of Catholic Bishops. "The Challenge of Peace: God's Promise and Our Response." In *A Pastoral Letter on War and Peace*. Washington, D.C.: USCC/Office of Publishing and Promotion Services, 1983.

Nuttall, Geoffrey. *Christian Pacifism in History*. Oxford: Basil Blackwell and Mott Ltd., 1971.

Oderberg, David. "Teaching Tradition." *National Review* (May 3, 2005), https://www.nationalreview.com/2005/05/teaching-tradition-david-s-oderberg/.

O'Donovan, Oliver. *The Just War Revisited*. Cambridge: Cambridge University Press, 2003.

Omar, A. Rashied. "The Right to Religious Conversion: Between Apostasy and Proselytization." *Kroc Institute Occasional Paper* (August 2006), http://www.nd.edu/~krocinst/ocpapers/op_27_1.pdf.

Orr, Ralph. "War in the Old Testament." http://www.wcg.org/lit/ethics/war02.htm.

People of Praise Community "Summer Life in Allendale." *Vine and Branches Magazine* (August, 2007). http://www.peopleof-praise.org/thevine/.

—— "Our New City in Allendale." *Vine and Branches Magazine* (March 2006), http://www.peopleofpraise.org/thevine/.

—— "Missionary Stories from Indianapolis." *Vine and Branches Magazine* (November 2007), http://www.peopleofpraise.org/thevine/.

—— "In Kingston: Face to Face." *Vine and Branches Magazine* (January 2008), http://www.peopleofpraise.org/thevine/.

——"City-Building Plans in Portland." *Vine and Branches Magazine* (May-June 2006), http://www.peopleofpraise.org/thevine/.

Pope Benedict XV. "Spiritus Paraclitus." http://www.papalencycli-cals.net/Ben15/b15spiri.htm.

Pope Francis. "The Disgrace of War." https://w2.vatican.va/content/francesco/en/cotidie/2016/documents/papa-francesco-cotidie_20160920_the-disgrace-of-war.html

Pope John Paul II. Address to members of the Italian Religions Television Channel *Telespace,* March 22, 2003.

———— General Audience, July 21, 1999.

Pope Paul VI. 1975 Vatican "Statement on Disarmament." http://www.vatican.va/holy_father/paul_vi/messages/peace/documents/hf_p-vi_mes_19751018_ix-world-day-for-peace_en.html.

Powers, Gerard. "Catholic Peacebuilding: Moving Beyond Just War vs. Pacifism." *Prism* (Winter 2008): 13-14.

———— Personal Letter. November 1, 2008.

Presbytery of Greater Atlanta. "A Call for Conversation: Nonviolence and Abolition of War." http://www.presbyteryofgreateratl.org/ministry_teams/outreach/peacemaking/alternativepaper-Maydraft.htm.

Ranaghan, Kevin and Dorothy Ranaghan. *Catholic Pentecostals.* Mahway, NJ: Paulist Press, 1969.

Rasmussen, Larry, Reinhold Niebuhr Professor of Social Ethics at Union Theological Seminary. Unpublished statement on the World Trade Center attack. September, 2001.

Ratzinger, Josef, Cardinal. http://foro.univision.com/univision/board/message?board.id=politicaeneeuu&message.id=48631.

Richards,Leyton. *Christian Pacifism After Two World Wars: A Critical and Constructive Approach to the Problems of World Peace* (London: Independent Press, 1948)

Riley-Smith, Jonathan. "Holy Violence Then and Now: A historian looks at the causes and lingering effects of Christian warfare: an interview with Riley-Smith." *Christianity Today* (October 1, 1993), http://www.ctlibrary.com/3995.

Rinehart, James F. *Apocalytic Faith and Political Violence; prophets of terror.* London: Palgrave Macmillan, 2011.

Robbins, Carla Anne. "Thinking the Unthinkable: A World Without Nuclear Weapons." *New York Times* (June 30, 2008), https://www.nytimes.com/2008/06/30/opinion/30mon4.htm.

Roberts, Tom. "A Man for the World." *National Catholic Reporter* (November 9, 2007), http://www.natcath.org/NCR_Online/archives2/2007d/110907/110907a.htm.

—— Legacy of Pacifism anchors movement." *The Free Library,* https://www.thefreelibrary.com/Legacy+of+pacifism+anchors+movement.-a0182977332.

Robinson, James Harvey. *Readings in European History.* Boston: Ginn and Co., 1904.

Romero, Bishop Oscar. *The Violence of Love,* ed. James Brochman. San Francisco: Harper and Row, 1988.

Schaff, Phillip, et.al. *Nicene and Post-Nicene Fathers.* Series II. Volume XIV. New York: Cosimo, 1900, 2007.

Seelye, Katharine Q. "Pastor Urges His Flock to Bring Guns to Church." *New York Times* (June 26, 2009): A1.

Sider, Ronald J. "A Call for Evangelical Nonviolence." *Christian Century* (September 15, 1976): 755.

Simpson, Gary. *War, Peace and God: Rethinking the Just War Tradition.* Minneapolis: Augsburg/Fortress, 2007.

Spohn, William. *What are they saying about Scripture and Ethics?* New York: Paulist Press, 1985.

Stassen, Glen, ed. *Just Peacemaking: Ten Practices for Abolishing War.* Cleveland: The Pilgrim Press, 1998.

Swift, Louis J. *The Early Fathers on War and Military Service.* Wilmington, DE: Michael Glazier, 1983.

Tannehill, Robert C. "The Focal Instance as a form of New Testament Speech: A study of Matthew 5-39b-42." *Journal of Religion* (1979): 379.

Tertullian. "On Idolatry." *Ante-Nicene Fathers.* Edited by Alexander Roberts. Grand Rapids, MI: Eerdman, 1965, 3:73.

Valliere, Paul. *Holy War and Pentecostal Peace.* New York: The Seabury Press, 1983.

Volf, Miroslav. *Exclusion and Embrace.* Nashville, TN: Abingdon Press, 1996.

Wallace, Jim. "Contesting a theology of war confessing Christ in a world of violence." *Catholic New Times* (December 5, 2004). Highbeam Research, https://www.highbeam.com/doc/1G1-126073950.html.

Webb, Jim. *A Time to Fight.* Oregon: Broadway Books, 2008.

Wink, Walter. *Engaging the Powers.* Minneapolis: Fortress Press, 1992.

Winn, Albert Curry. *Ain't Gonna Sudy War No More.: Biblical Ambiguity and the Abolition of War.* Louisville, KY: Westminster/Jon Knox Press, 1993.

Wong, Rev. Dr. Gordon. "Pacifism or Peace? War, Peace and Justice in the Old Testament." *Church and Society.* http://www.ttc.edu.sg/csca/CS/2002-Aug/Pacifism%20or%20Peace.pdf.

Wright, N.T. *Jesus and the Victory of God.* Minneapolis: Augsburg/Fortress, 1996.

—— *Evil and the Justice of God.* Downers Grove, IL: IVP Books, 2006.

—— "God, 9/11 the Tsunami, and the New Problem of Evil." Transcript of lecture to the Church Leaders' Forum, Seattle Pacific University (May 18-19, 2005), http://spu.edu/depts/uc/response/summer2k5/features/evil.asp.

—— Interview. http://www.hornes.org/theologia/travis-tamerius/interview-with-n-t-wright.